DYSLEXIA AND OTHER LEARNING DIFFICULTIES

A Parent's Guide by Maria Chivers

Need
— 2 —
Know

GW00367460

First published in Great Britain in 2004 by
Need2Know
Remus House
Coltsfoot Drive
Peterborough
PE2 9JX
Telephone 01733 898103
Fax 01733 313524
www.need2knowbooks.co.uk

Large Print Edition 2010 (based on 2004 edition, with revisions in 2009).

Need2Know is an imprint of Forward Press Ltd.
www.forwardpress.co.uk

Contents

Chapter 22

Contributors

Dr David Cowell

B.Sc. M.Phil. Ph.D. Dip Psych.

David Cowell trained as a psychologist at the Tavistock Centre, London, before moving to work in the North of England. He was senior psychologist in Swindon for 18 years, but is now an independent consultant specialising in child and adolescent problems. He has an M.Phil. and Ph.D. from Exeter University and has written or contributed to a number of books. He has participated in many radio and television programmes.

Dr Richard Eyre

Consultant in Child and Adolescent Psychiatry

Dr Richard Eyre is a member of the Royal College of Psychiatrists and is a consultant in Child and Adolescent Psychiatry at Princess Margaret Hospital in Swindon. Having completed higher training at the Maudsley and Kings College Hospitals, he developed interests in adolescent psychiatry and family therapy. As a consultant psychiatrist in Richmond (1991-94), he worked closely with the Local Authority's Social Services Department and Education Department in developing inter-agency approaches to child protection issues and children with educational difficulties associated with school-based problems such as poor behaviour and attendance. In Swindon he is now responsible particularly for special services for children under the age of eight.

Keith Holland

B.Sc. FBCO. DCLP.

Keith is an optometrist practicing in Cheltenham, Gloucestershire, with a special interest in vision and learning. Over the last 20 years he has built up one of the largest specialist practices in Europe, dealing with the visual problems associated with dyslexia and learning difficulties. His practice has twice been awarded the title 'Specialist Eye Care Practice of the Year' and also 'The Children's Eye Care Practice of the Year'. Keith has published many articles on the links between vision and literacy and lectures widely on the subject, both at home and abroad. He is founder and chairman of the British Association of Behavioural Optometrists, a professional special interest group that represents practitioners around Britain working in this field. He is married and has four children.

Christine Robinson (nee MANN)

DBO. SRO.

Christine was born and educated in Birmingham, England. She trained as an orthoptist at the Children's Hospital, Birmingham, and worked from 1964 at the Princess Margaret Hospital, Swindon, recently transferring to the new Great Western Way Hospital, Swindon. Christine is married and has three sons, two of whom are dyslexic. She has had an interest in dyslexia for the last 20 years and enjoys assessing and helping children who are dyslexic. It is very useful to be able to see the problems from two different perspectives – a parent of dyslexic children and as a professional who is able to advise and treat.

A note of thanks

I would like to express my thanks to all the staff at the Swindon Dyslexia Centre, in particular to Deirdre Holland who inspired me many years ago, and for their continued help and support not just in preparing this book, but for the help with running the centre.

Special thanks are also extended to the specialists who have contributed to this book:

- Dr D Cowell B.Sc. M.Phil. Ph.D. Dip. Psych.
- Dr R Eyre – consultant in Child and Adolescent Psychiatry.
- Keith Holland B.Sc, FBCO, DCLP.
- Christine Robinson DBO, SRO.
- The British Dyslexia Association.

Disclaimer

This book is for general information about dyslexia and other learning difficulties. It is not intended to replace professional medical advice. It can be used alongside medical advice, but anyone concerned about their child is strongly advised to consult their GP.

I'm Not Marking This Mess

I can see his face ready to blow

he shouts so the whole class will know

'Sir, Sir I'm stuck, I need more time.'

'I told you what to do, don't step out of line.'

I find it hard and embarrassing with him yelling

about my reading writing and spelling.

'Hurry up, get on with it, I'm not marking this mess'

I say, 'I need more time, I'm doing my best'.

He tells me little kids can do better than me

'I've seen better from my daughter, she's only three

where's your full stops and capital letters?

Now go and sit down until you do better.'

It's hard to do my work I find

I never rest, it's always on my mind

then I get frustrated, rude and angry

because he doesn't understand me.

By Mark Chivers (12)

September 1995.

Reprinted by kind persmission of The Inner Hurt.

Introduction

Please teacher,
if I can't learn by the way you teach,
please teach me the way I learn

Extract from a poem

Millions of children go to school. The majority get along in the educational system with no problems. However, for some children who have special needs, it appears to be the start of an ongoing battle. These children usually need special education which often takes years to identify and costs a great deal of money.

Parents, particularly mothers, feel a sense of loss when their children first start school. Most children are also anxious but then the eagerness to absorb the wonders of school and all the avenues that open up comes into being. Sadly, for some parents a few months later, their dreams and aspirations are shattered. Their children do not seem to be on the same level with other children in class. Their classmates seem to be racing ahead.

Waiting for your child after school each afternoon seems fraught with problems. As the other children come pouring into the playground, clutching their reading folders, your child throws his arms around you for a hug and you hear the other mothers saying 'Another new book today, how wonderful'. Looking at your child's folder, you realise that your child is still on the same one. You try not to show your disappointment because you are fully aware that intelligence is not based only on reading. (But try telling the other mothers that!)

For several years you are encased in a vicious circle. Teachers appear to take it personally when your child does not read or write along with his peers. As with anything, it may take one child several years to read and another just a few weeks. Some children actually go to school reading.

After your child has been at school for a short time, this difference can be very clearly seen. Parents continue to voice their concerns to the class teacher, only to be fobbed off with 'He'll catch up'. The longer it goes on, the worse it gets. Relationships with teachers deteriorate, until in the end it seems like a constant battle of us and them. The teachers label you as 'troublesome' or 'over-anxious' parents and, as the relationship continues to crumble, your child senses this anxiety. Many parents who find themselves in this position say that school is a battlefield.

Some of the reasons for your child falling behind at school can include difficulty with:

■ reading, writing or number work.

■ speaking, hearing or sight.

■ a physical or mental disability.

■ emotional or behavioural problems.

■ medical or health problems.

You may, as parents, be asking yourselves where you can go for help and what your legal rights are. Throughout the country there are many organisations and publications that exist to help parents – but do you know where to find them?

Parents are often at the end of their tether when they call for help. In many cases if they asked for advice from the right people earlier, the problems could have been sorted out much more quickly. These difficulties often result in great frustration, not only for parents and teachers but also for the child, who falls even further behind and loses more self-esteem with each day.

This book is written in an easy-to-follow format. It aims to point you in the right direction in order to get the appropriate help and support in the quickest possible time, avoiding the sense of failure for your child and the pain and frustration for you, the parents.

I Know There is Something Wrong – But No One Will Listen! (1)

Every mother knows when there is something wrong with her child. This happened to me when my eldest son, Jeremy, started school. It is extremely frustrating to be told that the child is just naughty, lazy, slow or will not listen. Many of these children are desperately unhappy as they go through their school life being at the bottom of the class, knowing the answers but never being able to put them on paper.

Within a few months of Jeremy starting school, I started to talk to his teacher about his slow progress. I knew he was not learning at the same pace as the other children in his group. His friends would be reading different books almost every day but he would be reading the same one for months. Why? I knew he was intelligent but why couldn't he read?

He still couldn't recognise his own name!

When he was nearly seven, he still could not recognise his own name. Each time he changed classes after the summer holidays, he couldn't even find his name on the coat peg in the lobby.

I knew that something had to be done, but I didn't know what to do. Every few weeks I would go and see his teacher and tell them how worried I was. But repeatedly, and by several different teachers, I was told that 'boys are slower than girls' and 'he will catch up.' With niggling at the back of my mind, I knew that this was wrong!

What should I do?

Like many parents, I felt if I kept saying something was wrong and something needed to be done, it would cause a lot of bad feeling and they might take it out on my child. I didn't know what to do or who to turn to.

Friends said go to the headmistress – but I had spoken to her so many times since Jeremy had been at school and it was not getting any better. Perhaps he really was slow or backward! Perhaps he would never catch up!

It was at that time that a very good friend (and a teacher at this same school) said to me, 'What does it matter if he doesn't amount to anything? You will love him just as much, no matter what he does. At the end of the day, education isn't everything.'

Of course I would love him no matter what he did but that wasn't the point. I believe a mother's love is unconditional. A mother's duty is to protect and provide the best she can for her child. As long as a child does his best then it is irrelevant if her child fails – because he only fails in the eyes of others. But if a child is bright and fails to achieve his potential, then you are failing him if you don't do anything about it.

Was I just an over-anxious mother who expected far too much of him? But then what parent wouldn't be anxious with a child who couldn't read at nearly seven years of age? No matter how many times I tried to talk to the teaching staff, no one would listen. We were due to move to another part of the country in a few months and I wanted to try and sort the problem out before the move. How was I going to go about it?

Coming home from school with Jeremy one day, I could tell something was worrying him. As we walked along the road he started to get very upset, saying 'he wasn't the same as the other children, he couldn't read new books or do his maths work'. Finally, distraught with worry, I decided I was going to do something about it.

What was I to do now?

I knew who the educational psychologist was for our area and I contacted him. After explaining the position, he agreed to go into the school that week to carry out some tests. I was too frightened to tell the headmistress! The psychologist confirmed my fears. My son was very bright – but performing well below his ability. He was dyslexic. The psychologist said a plan of action was needed immediately to stop him falling further behind.

Later I was summoned to see the headmistress who was furious at being upstaged in this manner and accused me of going behind her back. I tried to explain that I had been asking for their help for three years and was getting nowhere. She refused to listen and stated that I had made a big mistake and that my son would always be labelled as backward. I knew my son was not backward but there was little point in discussing the matter any further, so I left the office feeling very guilty and worried that I may indeed have caused Jeremy a problem.

As soon as I spoke to the psychologist, however, he assured me that I had done the right thing. He explained that some schools were reluctant to call in the professionals and it was best to get the problems sorted out before they got worse. (I have since been told by several children that finding out they were dyslexic was fantastic, because before the diagnosis they had always thought they were thick.)

It was many years later that I realised that I had infuriated the headmistress through my own naivety, because there is a procedure that parents should follow – and that does not involve keeping the head in the dark!

While waiting for the written report from the educational psychologist to come through, we moved out of the area. My son had only been at his new school for a few weeks and the headmaster had already noticed there was a problem and was prepared to do something about it! The relief was overwhelming.

When the report came, it clearly showed that our son had specific learning difficulties (SpLDs). What on earth did that mean? How could I help? Who else could help and where could I find them? What was the school obliged to do and were they going to do it? The report had raised as many questions as it had answered.

Incidentally, up to that point, my county's psychologist service refused to put dyslexia on their reports. This has now been changed, although I understand there are still a few counties that are reluctant to do so.

Seeking help

My first point of call was the library, and the staff their were extremely helpful. If ever you are desperate to know where to start looking for help, find a good librarian, especially one that's worked in the area for several years. They are worth their weight in gold!

They suggested contacting the British Dyslexia Association as SpLDs often come under the 'dyslexia' heading. The local association explained there were various ways of having your child assessed, one was an educational psychologist's report. The other was an assessment carried out by specialist teachers aimed at identifying areas of weakness and strengths. Once a report was available, an Individual Education Plan (IEP) could be put in place for the school to work around.

Jeremy was offered a place locally with the Dyslexia Association and started attending weekly classes for an hour, and the improvement was quite dramatic. Within a very short period of time, his confidence started to increase because he could see all the other children had the same problems. He realised he was not alone. And I knew that the people working in this group were all dedicated to the children and, in almost every case, had first hand experience. Many, many times during the last 20 years, I have had cause repeatedly to thank Deirdre Holland of the Swindon Dyslexia Association and the librarians who gave me the help and pointed me in the right direction. (You can usually find a local branch of the British Dyslexia Association in your area, who will be more than pleased to help you.)

What on earth is a statement?

It was about this time that the school started to talk to us about our other son Mark, who was also falling behind at school. The school explained that they wanted to put a statement on him. Here we go again! What on earth was a statement? It sounds like some official document that you get in the courts or something, doesn't it?

The statementing process simply means putting a Statement of Educational Needs in place. In other words, formally identifying a problem to inform the school and other professional services of the child's needs. (see chapter 11).

I worked very closely with the school and other professionals, and Mark's Statement of Educational Needs came through very quickly. Some parents call our helpline (at the Swindon Dyslexia Centre) and say that in some cases it takes years to get a statement. This is against government guidance and is usually because the formal procedures are not put into place. Some people leave matters to go on far too long before they formally ask for tests to be carried out.

Is there light at the end of the tunnel?

Yes, yes and yes again. Over the years, both my children have made fantastic progress and are now average/above average in most areas. Jeremy has completed his HND at university for Information Technology and is now a network administrator for a national company. Mark qualified as a cabinet maker and works for one of the most prestigious firms in the country. So if you feel down about your child, there is light at the end of the tunnel – don't give up!

The local Dyslexia Association was keen to get me involved with the dyslexia movement and after a lot of help and advice, I opened an organisation called the Swindon Dyslexia Centre for people suffering with dyslexia, dyscalculia and dysgraphia/specific learning difficulties (SpLDs). We have a team of specialist teachers, psychologists, occupational therapists and physiotherapists. We are open full time and have approximately 100 students who come to us for individual help for one or two hours a week. Besides specialist teaching, we carry out several hundred diagnostic assessments and educational psychologist reports each year.

Since our helpline was set up a few years ago, we have helped thousands of people from all over the country and in some cases further a field: America, Africa, Australia, New Zealand and so forth. The parents who telephone say they feel so isolated, that they don't know where to go or who to turn to. We can give independent advice on dyslexia/SpLDs.

Most of these parents are desperate and at their wits end to know what to do about their child. If there is not a helpline in your area, how about setting one up? Many parents have the same worries as you do – so you can all support each other (see chapter 22).

Some schools tell parents that their child would have to move to a special school if their child received a Statement of Education. This conflicts with what the Department of Education says. In the vast majority of cases children stay at the same school.

Having received many thousands of calls over the last decade, I realised that there is plenty of help and information available but the problem is finding it.

The Department for Children, Schools & Families (DCSF) has many excellent leaflets on special educational needs (SEN), but many parents say, 'What is the DCSF?' As this information is available free to all parents, why is it not available in the foyer of every school?

Questions, questions, questions?

- Where can I get help?

- What help is available?

- How do you start looking for information?

- What is dyslexia, dyscalculia and dysgraphia?

- What is dyspraxia?

- What is attention deficit hyperactivity disorder (ADHD)?

- What is a Statement of Educational Needs? Should my child have one?

- If he has a statement, will he have to go to a special school?

- What is my child legally entitled to?

- What is the LEA (Local Education Authority)?

- What is the DCSF (Department for Children, Schools & Families) and where can I find them?

- And on and on …

At the Swindon Dyslexia Centre, these are the sorts of questions we are repeatedly asked. Although the government has an Education Advisory Service, parents do not know where it is. They produce many different booklets about special educational needs (SEN) but parents are left in awe of the vast array of books. Indeed, in many instances, you have to be widely educated yourself to make head or tail of the information. You also need to know where to get this information from in the first place.

It was at this point that I realised it would be helpful to all concerned if the information was available in one book. It aims to explain briefly what help is available and where parents can turn to for help and guidance. It is not an in-depth medical book on the types of disorders, but a guide to a few of the hidden handicaps that afflict us.

Summing Up

If you think there is something wrong with your child, then there probably is. Don't be put off with excuses that boys are slower than girls, they'll soon catch up or that the school does not have sufficient money to offer extra help. Be assertive, not aggressive, and ask for reading and spelling tests to be carried out. If the teacher says your child's reading level is 2, ask him what the reading 'age' is so that you can understand it better. Depending on the results of these tests, you may have to ask the school for a full assessment or an educational psychologist's report.

Special Educational Needs – Square Pegs into Round Holes! (2)

Special needs education covers a wide range of problems from simple hearing or visual difficulties, through the broad spectrum of handicaps both physical and physiological, to some of the severest handicaps i.e. mental handicap. Highly gifted children also come under this category and many parents of these children feel that they are often denied the monies desperately needed for their education.

There are hundreds and thousands of children struggling to come to terms with their education. Square pegs in round holes; it is very difficult for them to fit into the normal education field.

A lot of people suffer with learning difficulties, many of which are never recognised properly. Many of the disruptive children in schools are naughty simply because they do not fit into the system of sitting, watching and listening that prevails in the majority of education establishments.

These children need more help than the average child, bringing in the problem of extra cost. The average child is allocated 'x' number of pounds for their education, but the children who do not fit into this equation cost the government many, many times more.

Will the schools identify a problem?

The biggest problem seems to be identifying exactly what a special educational need (SEN) is. One school will identify the problems early and start to put in the necessary help. Others will use delaying tactics for years, knowing that eventually the problems will have to be dealt with by another school, college, etc, when the child moves on. Some Local Education Authorities (LEAs) are very good at recognising a child who has problems in the first year or two at school, others are not so good.

Some teachers still believe that if children are born into families where there are lots of books, and where adults and other children enjoy reading, children will automatically learn to read. It is their belief that the child slowly builds up the necessary connections between what we say and the marks on a piece of paper. However, for one reason or another, some children cannot seem to pick up these skills automatically and need extra help.

In this book, I have explained in some detail a few of the hidden handicaps that are difficult to see and therefore difficult to assess. Attention deficit hyperactivity disorder (ADHD) is probably the most notable as teachers and other parents often see it as children who are just spoilt because they are often so naughty.

Summing Up

Special educational needs covers a wide range of difficulties. The biggest problem is identifying exactly what the problem is. Without this it is difficult to put in the correct and necessary help to support the child.

Most children stay in mainstream schooling with some additional help, hardly any go to special schools.

Dyslexia – Specific Learning Difficulties (SpLDs) (3)

Dyslexia (pronounced dis-lex-ia) and specific learning difficulties (SpLDs) often come under the same umbrella which can cause confusion, especially among parents.

Dyslexia/SpLDs affects approximately 10% of the population, 4% severely.Problems can show themselves in reading, writing, number work, short-term memory, hand control and visual processing. Timekeeping, sense of direction and interpersonal skills can also be affected.

These difficulties often result in great frustration, bearing in mind that dyslexics are usually of average intelligence (many having even higher levels).

It used to be thought that dyslexia affected more males than females. However, there has been a lot of speculation recently that the numbers are probably equal. It is thought that girls are not being identified as much as boys because they are usually a lot quieter and are therefore simply not being diagnosed. Many of these children are extremely bright in lots of ways, always talking and asking questions. And yet they do not seem to reach their full potential in the academic field. A very good definition of dyslexia is by Dr J E Cullis who wrote:

'Dyslexia means having difficulty with words in reading, spelling and writing – in spite of having normal intelligence and ability'.

Dr J E Cullis, 1992.

Dyslexia was identified over a century ago, yet little was found out about the causes of dyslexia until about 30 years ago.

One of the earlier assumptions was that dyslexia was a middle class disease. This came about because people from the 'middle income' bracket could afford to have their children tested for dyslexia, which left people from disadvantaged backgrounds being labelled as slow or backward.

Thankfully, these assumptions no longer exist due to a plethora of research being carried out into the causes of dyslexia. It is now accepted in medical circles that the dyslexic brain is different. It is now indisputable that dyslexia is a neurological condition whose symptoms are most often demonstrated with difficulties in reading, writing, spelling and sometimes numeracy.

I believe one of the major advances in dyslexia will be made in the area of genetics and it may not be too long before babies are tested at birth, thereby enabling help to be given at a very early age.

Dyslexia is a registered disability under the Chronically Sick & Disabled Persons Act 1970, Education Act 1993 and the Disability Discrimination Act 1995.

Early identification has got to be the key, because once you identify that a child has a learning difficulty and rule out any medical problems, you can start working towards a solution.

Dyslexia in children

Early identification checklist

The signs below may indicate that a pre-school child is dyslexic – they do not need to have all of these problems. However, if these problems continue beyond the time that the average child has grown out of them, they may indicate dyslexia and advice should be sought.

Weaknesses

■ Is there a family history of learning difficulties?

■ Does the child have delayed or unclear speech, or a lisp?

- Does he have problems getting dressed, putting shoes on the correct feet and doing up buttons, laces, etc?

- Does he enjoy hearing stories but shows no interest in the written word?

- Do people continually say he is lazy and not paying attention?

- Does he have problems when skipping, hopping or playing with a ball?

- Does he bump into things and trip over a lot?

- Can he clap a rhythm back?

- Does he often accidentally say that blue is green, red is yellow, etc?

- Does he often have to search for words and often mislabel them?

- Does he confuse under/over and up/down?

- Can he select the odd word out from lists, for example cat, mat, pig, fat?

- Can he put things in sequence like numbers up to 10, days of the week and the alphabet?

- Using coloured beads, can he thread green, red, blue and white correctly?

- Does he grip pencils and pens too tightly?

Strengths

- Is he quick thinking and does he have a lot of original thought?

- Is he good at creating things and art?

- Does he have an aptitude for construction games: Lego, blocks, remote control, keyboards?

- Does he appear bright but unable to do simple things?

Children's checklist

The signs below may indicate a child is dyslexic – they do not need to have all of these problems. However, if these problems continue beyond the time that the average child has grown out of them, they may indicate dyslexia and advice should be sought.

Reading and spelling

When your child reads and spells, does he frequently:

- Confuse letters that look similar: d - b, u - n, m - n?

- Confuse letters that sound the same: v, f, th?

- Reverse words: was - saw, now - won?

- Transpose words: left - felt?

- Read a word correctly but then read it wrong further down the page?

- Change the words around: the cat sat on the mat (the mat sat on the cat)?

- Confuse small words: of, for, from?

- When reading, has difficulty in keeping the correct place on a line and frequently loses his place?

- Read correctly but does not understand what he is reading?

Writing

Even after frequent instruction does he still:

- Not know whether to use his right or left hand?

- Leave out capital letters or use them in the wrong places?

- Forget to dot the 'i's and cross 't's?

- Form letters and numbers badly?

- Slope his writing even when using margins and guide lines?

- Use punctuation and paragraphs in the wrong places, or not at all?

Other indications

- Is there a family history of dyslexia or similar difficulties?

- Was he a late developer?

- Is he easily distracted or have poor concentration?

- Does he get confused between: left/right, east/west, up/down, over/under?

- Does he have sequencing difficulties?

- Does he hold a pen too tightly and awkwardly?

- Does he have problems telling the time?

- Does he have problems with tying shoe laces, etc.?

- Does he have short-term memory problems relating to printed words and instructions?

- Does he have mixed laterality (i.e. uses either right or left hands/eyes in writing and other tasks)?

- Does he have particular difficulty copying from a blackboard?

- Does he show confusion with mathematical symbols (plus/minus, etc)?

- Does he have an inability to follow more than one instruction at a time?

- Is he unable to use a dictionary or telephone directory?

Adult dyslexia

Dyslexic people are often highly creative and original. They usually succeed through sheer hard work and determination; they are valuable members of a working team.

Many dyslexics excel in areas such as:

- Architecture.

- Arts.

- Computer sciences.

- Construction.

- Electronics.

- Engineering.

- Entertainment.

- Mathematics.

- Physics.

- Sport.

A high proportion of self-made millionaires are dyslexic, probably because they had the tenacity and self-belief to succeed (study by the Tulip Financial Group 2003).

Many adults who have dyslexia have never been diagnosed as being dyslexic. It is only now that some of them are coming to realise that they have a recognised problem and are seeking help.

Dyslexics often have major problems in a work environment, filling in forms, etc because they try to hide the problem. Many adults suffer from low self esteem, lack of confidence and fall short of their employment ability; they are often relieved to know their lack of progress is due to dyslexia and, once diagnosed, they can receive the right kind of help.

Dyslexia comes under the Disability Act (see chapter 20). However, many employers still fail to get the best from their staff, simply because they do not know how to assist them with their individual problems. The British Dyslexia Association has an essential information pack for employers: 'An Employer's Guide to Dyslexia'. This offers information and advice about dyslexia in the workplace and how to make reasonable adjustments.

Adult's checklist

Some of the problems listed below may indicate you have dyslexia, but you do not need to have all of them. Do you:

- Have a family history of dyslexia?
- Remember having problems when you were at school?

When reading do you:

- Take a long time?
- Have to re-read the same piece several times?
- Keep losing your place?
- Miss endings off words?
- Do you miss words out?
- Read correctly but not understand what you are reading?

When writing do you:

- Find it difficult to take notes?
- Produce 'messy work'?
- Not know 'where to start'?
- Have poor punctuation?
- Make lots of mistakes when spelling?
- Have good days and bad days with spelling?
- Miss endings off words?
- Reverse letters or leave them out?
- Have difficulty filling in forms, timesheets, etc?
- Have problems using a dictionary or telephone directory?
- Have problems recalling the months of the year, forwards and backwards?
- Have problems reading maps and directions?

- Have problems with left/right?
- Have problems with telling the time?
- Have problems with time management, getting to appointments on time, etc?

With numbers do you:

- Have difficulties with mental arithmetic?
- Reverse numbers or leave them out?
- Have problems repeating numbers backwards i.e., 863, 368?
- Mix up numbers i.e., 13 and 31?
- Often dial the wrong telephone numbers?
- Have problems doing sums in your head?

Summing Up

Special educational needs covers a wide range of difficulties. The biggest problem is identifying a need. Without this it is difficult to put in the necessary help to support the child.

Most children should be able to stay in mainstream school with some additional help.

Dyslexia does not stop you getting on in life. Look at the list below of just a few of the many successful dyslexic people.

Famous and successful dyslexics

- Hans Christian Andersen.
- Michael Barrymore.
- Dennis Bergkamp.
- Marlon Brando.
- Richard Branson.
- Cher.
- Agatha Christie.
- Winston Churchill.
- Margi Clark.
- Brian Connolly.
- Tom Cruise.
- Charles Darwin.
- Walt Disney.
- Thomas Edison.
- Albert Einstein.
- Whoopi Goldberg.
- Duncan Goodhew.

- Susan Hampshire.
- Carol Harrison.
- Goldie Hawn.
- Michael Heseltine.
- Jeremy Irons.
- Eddie Izzard.
- Lynda La Plante.
- Ruth Madoc.
- Michelangelo.
- Steve Redgrave.
- Richard Rogers.
- Jackie Stewart.
- Anthea Turner.
- Leonardo da Vinci.
- W B Yeats.
- Benjamin Zephaniah.

Dyslexia – Testing and Multi-Sensory Teaching (4)

If your child is giving some cause for concern, either because he is not performing at the same level as his peers or appears to be brighter than his peers but is not reaching his potential, then you can arrange for a dyslexia assessment.

Years ago, tests were only carried out after a child had reached seven years of age, or in many cases, even later. These days there are a variety of tests available from five and a half years of age and some even earlier. Some of these tests do not require a child to read or write.

Tests vary from 20 minutes to four hours. The shorter test has value as it can quickly and easily establish whether there is a problem and usually what is causing it. The most comprehensive of all is the educational psychologist's assessment.

All these tests give a good indication of the child's strengths as well as his weaknesses. They also show where the child is at the moment and what he is capable of performing. It is no good expecting a child to be top of the class if he is not able to reach that level, nor is it right that we should accept a child under performing if he is capable of doing better.

There are many different tests and assessments available today and I could not attempt to write about them all. I have listed the ones that I have used and that are well known in the field of dyslexia. The tests and assessments can range from £30 to £500.

Screening

- Aston Index Assessment 5 - 14 years
- Lucid Rapid Dyslexia Screening* 4 - 15 years

- Lucid CoPS Baseline (CoPS)* 4 - 8 years
- Lucid CoPS Baseline (CoPS)* 4 - 6 years
- Lucid CoPS Cognitive Profile System (CoPS)* 4 - 8:11 years
- LASS Junior* 8 - 11:11 years
- LASS Secondary* 11 - 15:11 years
- LADS (Lucid Adult Dyslexia Screening)* 16+
- LADS Plus (Lucid Adult Dyslexia Screening Plus) 15+
- Dyslexia Early Screening Test (DEST - 2) 4:6 - 6:5 years
- Dyslexia Screening Test (DST) 6:6 – 16:5 years
- Bangor Screening 8+ years
- Dyslexia Adult Screening Test (DAST) 16:5 years+
- Dyscalculia Screening Test 5 - 14 years
- Dyscalculia Screening Test - Steps Ahead in Dyscalculia Series.
- Educational Psychologist Report Any age
- Phonological Assessment Battery (PhAB) 6:00 - 14:11
- Phonological 3:00 - 6:11 Pipa
- Phonological 5:00 – 7:00 PAT

*The Lucid Screening Systems are available from Lucid and are fully computerised.

The DST products can be purchased from Pearson Assessment.

The Dyscalculia Screening Test – Steps Ahead Series is available from www.dyslexiaa2z.com.

A fuller description of these tests can be found in my book Practical Strategies for Living with Dyslexia.

An educational psychologist's assessment is the most comprehensive of all the tests available and also checks the student's intelligent quotient (I.Q.). Educational psychologists are available free through many schools, some colleges and universities. However, they will only be consulted if the school feels there is a long-term problem, and this may take a considerable time to arrange. You can see an educational psychologist privately in order to get your child's needs established quickly.

In the past, students had to have educational psychologists' reports carried out every year in order to receive grants. Recently these rules have changed. Instead of having a report carried out each year, the Department for Children Schools and Families (DCSF) is now saying that if a student has one (post 16) then he does not need to have another one. More information is available on the DCSF's website. Although a student may not be required to have additional reports, it is often in their own interest to do so. These reports are valuable, not only in assessing progress made but, what is often more important at this stage, identifying the student's need at the current time.

Can I get help to pay for an educational psychologist?

Some private insurance companies fund assessments by chartered psychologists. The referral has to be made via the doctor. It is advisable to speak to your insurance company before making an appointment.

Online dyslexia assessment

Short dyslexia screening assessments can be found online at a few organisations.

Three good sites are:

1. www.dyslexiaa2z.com – can be filled in online and is easy to use for all ages.

2. www.dyslexiacentre.co.uk – can be filled in online, split into different age groups and easy to use for all ages.

3. www.bdadyslexia.org – print out form then work out score.

These can be very useful in initially identifying a problem.

Online learning style assessment

Everyone has a preferred learning style. Knowing and understanding our learning styles helps us to learn more effectively. One assessment I found online was from www.ldpride.net. It gives a very useful tool to help you find out which way of learning is best for you. This is very useful when planning an individual learning plan. For instance, it could show something like this: tactile 41%, visual 32% and auditory 27%. The teacher can then plan a programme with the main emphasis on using tactile methods.

Multi-sensory teaching

Research has shown that using a structured multi-sensory approach is the best way for students with learning difficulties to successfully overcome their problems.

Multi-sensory means using different senses i.e. auditory, visual, voice and touch. Using an integrated multi-sensory approach, combined with memory, perceptual training and regular over-learning activities, ensures that the student achieves success and is able to participate fully in all areas of the National Curriculum.

As the problems are overcome, the student retains the additional abilities that are often developed to help cope with dyslexic problems. These can include highly developed memory for events, sounds and faces, unusual creative skills and exceptional ability in lateral thinking.

Well established successful teaching schemes such as Alpha to Omega, Hickey, Units of Sound, etc, as well as a wide range of educational games and computer based learning programmes, are used.

Audio books

When children start secondary school, one major concern for parents of dyslexic children is the amount of homework the child is given – especially with the amount of course textbooks.

Books in audio format make it easier for the student to comprehend and remember information because they do not have to decode the written text.

There are two charities now that supply textbooks on tape through the post: Calibre and Listening Books.

Once you register for membership, the company will send you a catalogue of all books on file and you can select tapes of your choice. All tapes are delivered by post.

Both these charities supply books for all ages.

Videos and DVDS

As students start to work towards their GCSEs, this is the time when it becomes all the more difficult for the dyslexic student. However, in the last few years, more and more work has been transferred to video and DVDs. Shakespeare's Romeo and Juliet, Macbeth and Othello are all available on DVD, which is helping students with dyslexia tremendously. One student said after studying the text, it was only when she saw the DVD that it all became clear.

Summing Up

As you can see there are a wide range of assessments and tests available for identifying dyslexia. Whichever one you choose, please remember that it is imperative to do so early. After identifying a special educational need, it is vital that teachers try to sort out the problems by using a multi-sensory teaching method.

Many parents say that they knew there was something wrong at a very early age, often when the child started playgroup or nursery.

Dyscalculia (5)

Dyscalculia (pronounced: 'dis-cal-qu-lee-ah') is a specific learning difficulty in mathematics. Like dyslexia, dyscalculia can be caused by a visual perceptual deficit. Dyscalculia refers specifically to the inability to perform operations in maths or arithmetic. It could be described as an extreme difficulty with numbers. Dyscalculia does not have the same stigma surrounding it, but it is very important to recognise it as soon as possible before it impacts on a child's self esteem. Just as there is no single set of signs that characterise all dyslexics, there is no one cause of dyscalculia.

We still do not know very much about this condition, however it is estimated 3 – 6%* of the population may have it. Around 60% of dyslexics have difficulties with dyscalculia. A lot of research is now taking place and it is hoped that over the next few years we will begin to understand this a little more. (*Badian, 1999; Gross-Tsur et al, 1996; Lewis et al, 1994).

Students may have difficulties with the simplest of numerical tasks, calculations and learning number facts (e.g. multiplication tables). They confuse larger numbers with smaller ones and have problems with simple counting. They often start answering a question and then divide instead of adding or multiply instead of taking away – literally forgetting what they are being asked to do. These factors are often exacerbated by poor processing and sequencing skills and short-term memory problems. They are usually good at answering verbally but cannot tell you how they got the answer.

The DfES defines dyscalculia in terms of:

'A condition that affects the ability to acquire arithmetical skills. Learners may have difficulty understanding simple number concepts, lack an intuitive grasp of numbers and have problems learning number facts and procedures.' DfES, Guidance to support pupils with dyslexia and dyscalculia, 2001.

Developing a student's skills with sequencing, space organisation, deduction, directional awareness, timekeeping and strategy are essential. The earlier it's started, the better.

Along with dyslexia, the extent to which you can be affected varies tremendously in each individual.

Dyscalculia checklist

Does your child frequently:

■ Confuse numbers i.e., 51 for 15?

■ Transpose and reverse numbers when reading or writing?

■ Confuse minus, subtract and take away?

■ Confuse add, plus and add on?

Does he have problems when:

■ Learning the times tables?

■ Working out simple money and change?

■ Estimating numbers?

■ Working out percentages?

■ Working out averages?

■ Understanding 2 + 5 = 7 and 5 + 2 = 7?

■ Working out the speed in miles per hour?

■ Telling the time?

■ Learning the date?

■ Describing how he got the answer to a mathematical problem?

Online dyscalculia test

A dyscalculia test is available from the Steps Ahead in Dyscalculia Scheme, (Cowell & Chivers, 2009) and can be found online at:

http://www.dyslexiaa2z.com/learning_difficulties/dyscalculia/
dyscalculia_test.html.

This can be very useful in initially identifying a problem. A workbook to go with the scheme is available in this series.

Summing Up

Dyscalculia may not have the same stigma surrounding it, yet it is very important that it is recognised as soon as possible. If these problems are not picked up at an early age, they impact on a child's self-esteem and can take a long time to correct.

Dysgraphia (6)

Dysgraphia (pronounced: 'dis-graf-ia') is the inability to write properly, despite a student being given adequate time and attention.

The cause of this disorder is still unknown but it's thought it could be due to a language disorder and/or damage to the motor system. There is ongoing research to try to establish exactly what causes it and how people can be helped.

If people are suffering with dysgraphia, the main sign is that their handwriting will barely be legible. The writing will appear incorrect or distorted and have letters of different sizes and spaces. This could be a ploy because if someone cannot read your writing, they cannot tell if it is spelt properly! Some people with dyslexic-type problems may deliberately write scruffily so people cannot tell if it is spelt wrong. However, it is usually a problem with the actual physical side of writing.

There appears to be two types of dysgraphia:

1. *Phonological dysgraphia – writing words as a pure 'sound' spelling which is incorrect e.g. writing brought as 'brot' or station as 'stayshun'.

2. *Visual dysgraphia – writing words which are correctly spelt apart from some letters being reversed, e.g. drink as 'brink' or the bizarre, abnormal and irregular formation of letters. The words may sometimes look fine but they have been produced in an abnormal order of pen strokes.

*Dysgraphia 2.doc NINDS. June 2004.

Will exercise help?

Some people may benefit from exercises to improve fine motor control but for others, despite practising, the problems persist. Handwriting can be improved by regular practice and there are several very good books that may help: Handwriting Without Tears, Why Johnny Can't Write and The Handwriting Rescue Kit available from REM. Occupational therapy may also help.

Developing skills through play

Multi-sensory methods used when playing are the best way to learn.

Playing with things like:

- Practising letter formation in sand/salt trays. (I use cat litter trays – they are very cheap.)
- Using chalk or coloured pens to do letter formation on black/white board.
- Shape and pattern copying.
- Tracing.
- Using Spirograph to practise writing – write, shake it and it goes away.
- Colouring by number.
- Following the line to find out which rabbit belongs to which hutch.
- Threading coloured beads.
- Juggling.
- Swimming.

Some items have been found to be useful, including:

- Pencil grips – help to hold the pencil correctly.
- Templates – help to keep paper in the right place/angle.
- Pre-formed letter shapes – children follow with their fingers.

- Word prediction and speech synthesis software packages.

- Sloping Board Posture Pack (available from Back in Action).

- Dexball (uses 'a unique method to hold a pen' – Insight Medical Products).

Computer versus handwriting

The majority of students with dysgraphia may be able to perform better once they can use a computer. It means that they can concentrate on the actual content of their work rather than what it looks like and the sheer 'mechanics' of writing. I would not normally advocate very young children using computers instead of writing but I think there are always exceptions to the rule and it may be that the student would benefit from this.

However (before I am inundated with letters from teachers, all over the country), I still think children should practise handwriting every day. There are still occasions when we do not have a computer with us and there has been some research which supports the view that when we physically write things down, we remember the 'picture' of the spelling better. (How many times have you tried to spell something aloud and then written it down to check? When you do this it is the 'picture' of the word you are checking.)

Can software help?

There are various software packages to help with dysgraphia such as word prediction and speech synthesis software packages. These software packages can help if the only thing stopping a student getting the work down on paper is a physical problem. These programs do take a little getting used to but they save a lot of time, effort and frustration! (See chapter 13.)

Where can I get help with writing?

There are several groups that specialise in handwriting. One is the National Handwriting Association (NHA), formerly the Handwriting Interest Group or HIG. Their main concern is to promote the improvement of handwriting standards in schools and support children with handwriting difficulties.

Another excellent group is the Society for Italic Handwriting (SIC) which launched The Good Handwriting Initiative in 1997. The Society's aim is to promote good handwriting and good teaching. A particular concern is to help teachers at Key Stage 1 (KS1) who wish to begin teaching cursive writing from the first day in reception.

Practice makes perfect – not always!

I took years and years trying to develop neat handwriting – to no avail! The teachers used to say that 'it looked as if a spider had crawled out of my inkwell and all over the paper'. On one occasion I had to rewrite an essay six times because the teacher could not read it. In the end my mother refused to let me re-write it again.

At 14 I 'adopted' typewriting as my second form of writing (in those days that was very young). I realised that people could actually read what I was trying to write. In the mid 70s we did not have computers in school so I could not use it for my coursework at the time. (Nearly all schools allow computers to be used now.) At the end of the day, what is being tested? The quality of one's writing or the contents of the essay?

Until we know more about this very complex area, it is difficult to decide what is the most useful way to help the student with dysgraphia.

Signs of dysgraphia

Checklist

The signs below may indicate that someone has dysgraphia – they do not need to have all of these problems. However, if these problems continue beyond the time that the average person has grown out of them, they may indicate dysgraphia and advice should be sought.

- Written text is very poor considering language development.

- Poor motor control.

- Writing is almost impossible to read.

- Mixture of printing and cursive writing on the same line.

- Writing in all directions, i.e. right slant then left slant.

- Big and small spaces between words.

- Different sized letters on the same line.

- Mixture of capital letters and lower case letters on the same line.

- Abnormal and irregular formation of letters.

- Very slow writing.

- Very slow copying from board.

- Not following margins.

- Griping the pen too tightly and with a 'fist grip'.

- Holds pen very low down so fingers almost touch the paper.

- Watching hand intently while writing.

- Poor spelling.

- Bizarre spelling.

- Problems with spelling wrong words i.e. 'brot' for brought and 'stayshun' for station.

- Problems with spelling words, e.g. drink as 'brink'.

Dysgraphia workbook

A dysgraphia workbook is available from the 'Steps Ahead in Dysgraphia training System' (Cowell & Chivers 2009) and can be found online at: http://www.dyslexiaa2z.com/learning_difficulties/dysgraphia/dysgraphia_test.html

Summing Up

The problem of dysgraphia may have only recently been recognised but it is very important that we do not just leave it. It took over 100 years for people to start taking dyslexia seriously.

Maybe we should begin to make exceptions for the minority of people who find writing neatly almost impossible to do.

Dyspraxia (7)

Developmental Coordination Disorder (DCD) is a developmental disorder affecting motor coordination. In the UK these difficulties are usually referred to as dyspraxia. You may also hear the term 'perceptuo-motor dysfunction' and 'motor learning difficulties'.

It is not certain what causes dyspraxia but it is thought to be due to an immaturity in neurone development in the central nervous system.

Dyspraxia affects approximately 5-10% of the population, about 2% severely. The overwhelming majority of sufferers are male.

Like dyslexia and dyscalculia, the extent to which people are affected varies tremendously. Recent research suggests that 52% of children with dyslexia have features of dyspraxia (Kaplan 1998). Some people may be affected only slightly, others more seriously. Sometimes developmental milestones are delayed and there could be speech difficulties. This, not surprisingly, leads on to difficulties at school. Often this problem is accompanied by difficulties in vision and movement, i.e. problems with catching a ball.

The Medical Journal defines dyspraxia as:

'A serious impairment in the development of motor or movement coordination that can't be explained solely in terms of mental retardation or any other specific inherited or acquired neurological disorder.'

What a mouthful! I understand it to be:

'If they persistently continue to fall over and are clumsy well after the age their other friends stopped doing it'.

If you are concerned, you should talk to your doctor, health visitor or special needs co-ordinator at school (SENCO). You may be referred for an assessment to a number of specialists including a paediatrician, educational psychologist, physiotherapist, occupational therapist or speech therapist.

While there is yet no known treatment for dyspraxia, regular physiotherapy and/or occupational therapy may improve motor and coordination skills. Some children have also shown an improvement by taking fatty acid supplements such as Efalex and eye q (see chapter 18) although there is no firm evidence to support this.

Recent evidence shows that difficulties with dyspraxia do not stop in childhood but continue throughout life.

People with dyspraxia may also experience other problems such as dyslexia, dyscalculia, dysgraphia or attention deficit hyperactivity disorder (ADHD). Recent research suggests that 52% of children with dyslexia have features of dyspraxia (Kaplan 1998).

Further information can be obtained from the charity, the Dyspraxia Foundation.

Dyspraxia checklist

Following is a checklist for dyspraxia. However, you must remember that when children start school they may make several of the mistakes listed. It is only if these symptoms persist beyond the time that the average child has grown out of them that they may indicate dyspraxia and advice should be sought. All children who fall over, drop things and generally take longer to do things are not necessarily suffering with dyspraxia.

Infants

Very young children may have delayed milestones, including problems with:

■ Sleeping.

- Being fretful and fidgeting.
- Sitting up (keep falling over).
- 'Bum shuffling' rather than crawling.
- Learning to walk.
- Learning to talk.
- Eating sensibly.
- Baby puzzles or building blocks.
- Picking up small items.

Children

As opposite and generally:

- Fidgets constantly.
- Never sits still.
- When sitting, swings his legs and fiddles with his hands and anything else around him.
- Knocks things over.
- Spills things.
- Has problems using knives and forks.
- Bumps into objects all the time.
- Stumbles into doors.
- Falls over for no apparent reason.
- Has problems using stairs and steps.
- Has difficulties standing on tiptoe or one leg.
- Has problems dressing and doing up buttons.
- Has trouble doing shoelaces up.
- Has problems telling the time.

When playing, has problems with:

- Fine motor skills.

- Puzzles, construction games, Lego, etc.

- Using scissors and craft tools.

- Painting and colouring small areas.

- Threading a needle.

- Catching or kicking a ball.

- Hitting a moving ball, i.e. tennis, etc.

- Riding a bike.

- Using roller skates.

- Difficulties with swimming and the coordination needed.

In a more formal setting, i.e. a classroom, teachers may notice the following problems:

- When reading, has difficulty in keeping the correct place on a line and frequently loses his place.

- When writing, grips the pencil very tightly and awkwardly.

- When writing, changes hands constantly and does not know whether to use his right or left hand.

- Writes in different directions on the same paper.

- Does not use margins.

- Writing slopes on page.

- Has difficulty copying symbols, i.e. circles, squares and triangles.

- Has difficulty copying work from whiteboards, etc.

- Has difficulty following instructions.

- Has difficulty reading maps.

Summing Up

While there is still no known treatment for dyspraxia, physiotherapy and occupational therapy may help improve motor and coordination skills. There are lots of things you can do at home to help, for example balancing games, trampettes, wobble boards, standing on one leg, etc. Most importantly, these things are fun.

Attention Deficit Hyperactivity Disorder ADHD/ADD (8)

Attention deficit hyperactivity disorder (ADHD) has been known about for a long time. It has undergone several name changes, at one time being known as 'hyperkinesias' (Latin derivative for 'super active'), hyperactivity, attention deficit disorder (ADD) and latterly, ADHD (with or without hyperactivity). As with other problems mentioned in this book, there are different degrees of severity. Many children with ADHD display features of dyslexia and dyspraxia.

A child who can't concentrate, moves around constantly, has poor school performance (in contrast with his intelligence) and has disruptive behaviour may be suffering with ADHD. There is evidence to suggest that children with this problem could eventually be expelled from school and/or worse, be in trouble with the police. Until recently it was assumed that children would grow out of ADHD, however it is now known that over a third of children will continue to have symptoms in adulthood.

At times all children may be overactive and inattentive but hyperactive children are disruptive nearly all the time. ADHD is thought to affect between 3% and 7% of the school age population. While there is evidence to suggest that the overwhelming majority of children with ADHD are male, there is some research to suggest that this could be because girls often have the mainly inattentive form of the condition. This may show up as the child being quiet and dreamy and therefore they are not actually being identified as having ADHD.

Are there different types of ADHD?

There appears to be three subtypes of ADHD:

1. The predominantly hyperactive impulsive type.

2. The predominantly inattentive type.

3. The combined type (which makes up the majority of cases).

People with ADHD appear to be intensely restless and impulsive: if they think about something, they do it – sometimes with disastrous results! They have a hard time focussing on things and get bored after just a few minutes. They often find it difficult paying attention for the shortest possible time, thereby causing problems with organisation and completing routine tasks.

Diagnosing ADHD

In order to make a diagnosis of ADHD, the symptoms usually:

- Start before the child is seven years of age.

- Cause real problems in at least two areas of the child's life, i.e. school and home, work, etc.

- Are long-term.

When assessing for ADHD, it is important that everyone concerned with the child is given the chance to participate in the assessment. This comprehensive study should include:

- Family history.

- Behaviour as a baby – restless, noisy, screams, etc.

- Behaviour as a toddler.

- Medical development.

- Behaviour at pre-school.

- Behaviour at school.

- Behaviour at home (which can sometimes be worse or better).

For further information on ADHD check out an excellent book, ADHD - The Essential Guide (Need2Know).

Oppositional Defiant Disorder (ODD)

Many children with ADHD have oppositional defiant disorder (ODD). This disorder is defined by negative and disruptive behaviour, especially towards authority figures such as parents and teachers.

Who can help me with my child?

There are various ways and people who can help children with ADHD. These include:

- Psychotherapy.
- Cognitive Behaviour Therapy (CBT).
- Physiotherapy.
- Teacher training.
- Classroom support.
- Support groups for the children and their parents.

What can I do to help my child?

There are lots of ways of making things easier on your child and yourself. Some ways include:

- Praise, praise and praise.
- Try to ignore bad behaviour (when it is safe to do so).
- Always reward good behaviour.
- Make sure you are directly looking at the child and make eye contact when you speak to him.
- Give one instruction at a time.

Does medication work?

Some people think by giving medication to children suffering with these problems, they will become drug dependent. However, there appears to be little scientific support for this argument. Children who are deemed in need of medication after extensive tests should be given the opportunity of using it.

Medication, where appropriate, should only be used with other forms of treatment, i.e. psychotherapy, behaviour therapy, etc and should be re-assessed regularly. The most common form of medication used is methylphenidate (Ritalin). This type of medication is still seen by some groups as extremely controversial. However, if you are one of the many desperate parents who have tried every thing else, they are seen as a necessary evil.

Dextroamphetamine (Dexedrine, Adderall) used to be recommended but has now been withdrawn by the National Institute for Clinical Excellence (NICE).

Where can I get help for my child?

Sally Bundy, MBE is the founder and director of the Hyperactive Children's Support Group (HACSG). The group was founded by Mrs Bundy and her late mother, Mrs Vicky Colquhoun, to help people who found themselves in a similar situation to one they were experiencing some years ago.

It was in 1980 that Mrs Bundy and Mrs Colquhoun put forward a radical proposal to the medical profession, suggesting a link between people with ADHD and a lack of fatty acids in their diet.

They were the first people to take on the medical experts to prove that they knew more than them about the causes of hyperactivity in children.

The women, who had no scientific or medical qualifications, noted that children with hyperactivity or ADD often had other symptoms such as excessive thirst, dry skin and allergies. They carried out a survey of over 200 children with hyperactivity and concluded their problems were linked to biochemical imbalances. These were caused by a deficiency of Essential Fatty Acids (EFAs). Two of these fatty acids are supplied by evening primrose oil and it was noted that there was an improvement in hyperactivity by children who took the oil. The scientific establishment, however, never took it seriously.

After almost 15 years, an American journal of clinical nutrition confirmed Mrs Colquhoun and Mrs Bundy's findings. There has since been extensive research that has also confirmed their earlier findings that some dyslexic children can be helped with EFAs.

There are now several supplements available, two of which are Efalex and eye q, that contain these missing fatty acids. These supplements are available in liquid, tablet and 'chews', which make them much more palatable for children to take.

Mrs Bundy has continued to work tirelessly to raise awareness of ADHD and in 2005 she was awarded an MBE for her work. Further information is available on her group's excellent website, the Hyperactivity Children's Support Group (HACSG).

Another useful site is that of ADDISS, the National Attention Deficit Disorder Information and Support Service.

Case study

'My son Miles was born hyperactive and the only treatment offered was an endless succession of drugs, none of which were effective. Being unhappy about the long-term effect of these, I decided to try and find out all I could about this problem. It seems that in some cases hyperactivity is aggravated, if not caused, by intolerance to some chemical additives in food, notably colouring, flavouring and preservatives. Consequently, I eliminated these from his diet, with very encouraging results.'

Sally Bundy, MBE founder and director of Hyperactive Children's Support Group (HACSG).

The Mental Health Foundation has also published a free information booklet on ADHD.

Do artificial colourings in food cause behavioural problems?

After decades of debate concerning artificial food colourings in food and the link with children's bad behaviour, it was gratifying to see that the research carried out below finally appears to support the lobby against food colourings being added to our foods.

* In 1987 the HACSG, with the support of Professor Neil Ward, Senior Lecturer in Chemistry at the University of Surrey and the group's Scientific Director, found that, out of a total of 357 children who had been diagnosed as hyperactive, 87% had adverse reactions to artificial colourings and 72% to artificial preservatives in food.

*Hyperactive Children's Support Group – website home page

ADHD/ADD checklist

The signs below may indicate that a person has ADHD, but they do not need to have all of these problems. However, if these problems continue beyond the time that their peers have grown out of them, they may indicate ADHD and advice should be sought.

Infants

■ Often distressed.

■ Extreme restlessness.

■ Poor sleep pattern.

■ Difficult to feed.

■ Excessive and constant thirst.

■ Dry skin.

■ Frequent tantrums.

- Screaming.

- Head banging.

- Rocking the cot.

Children

- Generally fearless and impulsive.

- Does not stop to think.

- Takes undue risks.

- May dash around.

- May run out into roads.

- Erratic behaviour.

- Accident-prone.

- Increased activity – always on the go.

- Compulsive touching of everything and everyone.

- Clumsy.

- Talks incessantly.

- Allergies.

- Sleep and appetite problems continue.

Poor coordination:

- Difficulty tying laces.

- Difficulty dressing.

- Problems with handwriting.

- Difficulty with ball games.

- Lacks self-esteem.

- Problems with making friends.

- Impatience so they will not take turns in games.

- Demands must be met immediately.

- May hit out and grab things.

Inflexible personality:

- Un-cooperative.

- Defiant.

- Disobedient.

In a more formal setting, i.e. the classroom, teachers (as well as seeing the above mentioned behaviour) may notice the following problems:

- Poor concentration and brief attention span.

- Sitting through lessons is almost impossible.

- Fidgets constantly.

- Constantly moving feet, hands, etc.

- Taps pens, pencils, books, etc.

- Roams around classroom.

- Cannot take turns.

- Blurts out answers to questions.

- Speaks entirely inappropriately and out of turn.

- Has a weak short-term memory.

- Normal IQ but under-performs at school.

Adults

- Most of the features of ADHD in childhood remain.

- Employment may be difficult because of relationship problems and poor memory.

- Anti social behaviour may become so extreme it leads to trouble with the law and to excess alcohol consumption.

- Poor self-esteem may be distressing.

Summing Up

There has been a lot said over the years on the subject of ADHD, most of it negative, blaming parents and branding children as just being naughty. It has been over 25 years since a link with fatty acid deficiency was found and it is about time that there was a routine assessment available so all children can be tested for it.

Gifted Children (9)

I make no apologies for including the gifted child in this book. Although these children do not come into the special educational needs definition, their educational needs in many cases are still not being met. The fact that these children are gifted should mean that the LEAs have a duty to provide extra support for them – over and above their peer group.

There are various degrees of giftedness in the same way as there are varying degrees of learning difficulties. Some children are gifted in a particular area, i.e. maths, art or music, but in this chapter I am concentrating on children who are gifted overall.

In March 2004, David Bell, the government's chief inspector for Education, addressed the National Association for Able Children in Education, saying that gifted pupils should be put on a special educational needs register in the same way as those with learning difficulties. He went on to say that some primary schools in particular were failing to meet the needs of gifted pupils. If gifted students were put on a register, it would be easier to provide them with an Individual Education Plan (IEP) so they could be monitored regularly.

There still does not appear to be a standard way of identifying gifted children in our schools. All LEAs appear to be 'doing their own thing', some better than others.

Dr Peter Congden realised over 30 years ago the desperate need for gifted children to be identified, and set up the Gifted Children's Information Centre. Along with a few other organisations he has been working hard to bring this to the notice of the government's advisors. In 2002, some 30 years after Dr Congdon's work began, the government finally recognised what these agencies had been saying for years and set up the National Academy for Gifted and Talented Youth (NAGTY). This programme is now recognized as the Young Gifted and Talented programme. The Department for Children Schools and Families (DCSF) expects schools and colleges to identify their talented learners and put them forward to the YG&T programme.

National Academy for Gifted and Talented Youth (NAGTY)

The National Academy for Gifted and Talented Youth (NAGTY) opened in 2002 at Warwick University. Each year they run a summer school for over a thousand gifted children.

Millions of pounds have been put into this project in the hope that it will raise educational standards in the country and also identify the gifted child early. It is hoped that the scheme will improve self-esteem for gifted children, particularly from disadvantaged backgrounds.

What is the YG&T programme about?

The programme is designed to offer services which stretch and stimulate at least the top 10% of the brightest and most talented young learners in the country, engaging all gifted and talented learners aged 4-19 through a new Learner Academy. Further information is available from the Young Gifted and Talented website.

World-class tests for gifted children (world class arena)

During 2001 we saw the launch of new world-class tests that had been developed jointly by examiners in Britain, America, Australia, New Zealand and Hong Kong. The results will be used as an international benchmark for gifted children.

The tests are voluntary and are aimed at the top 10% ability range. Thousands of students around the world have now taken these tests, and the UK government is using the results to help fast-track gifted pupils through the school system.

Schools and colleges are encouraged to put children through these tests. However, it is important that the right students are put forward. Students should be able to think creatively, logically, use thinking skills to solve problems and demonstrate clearly how they think through and solve questions.

The World Class Arena has continued to grow and develop, and in 2004 materials were published to help education establishments. More information is available from the World Class Arena website.

Intelligent Quotient (I.Q.) tests

For parents who suspect their child is gifted, it is important to organise an independent psychologist's report. The child will take part in a lot of different tasks, after which you will receive a report listing your child's strengths and weaknesses and, more importantly, it will give you an I.Q. level for your child. When you have the results, schools can use the report to make an Individual Education Plan (IEP) for your child.

What exactly is giftedness?

There are different levels of giftedness in the same way as there are varying degrees of learning difficulties.

The following list gives a rough idea of the ranges of intelligence levels used by psychologists in the UK.

- Gifted I.Q.: over 130 = 3% of the population.
- Highly gifted I.Q.: over 140 = 0.6% of the population.
- Extremely gifted I.Q.: over 160 = 0.01% of the population.
- Profoundly gifted I.Q.: over 180 = 0.0001% of the population (just 60 people out of the UK population of 60 million).

There are many online companies that offer free basic I.Q. tests. One of the largest run every year in the UK is Test the Nation, run by the BBC. You can find it at www.bbc.co.uk/testthenation. These are very useful to take part in. Depending on the results, you may wish to take a more thorough test.

Gifted Children's Information Centre

In 1978, Dr Peter Congdon founded the Gifted Children's Information Centre. Its principal function is to publish and disseminate information on the subject of gifted and talented children. Over the years, as demand for publications and books has grown, Dr Congdon has addressed many international conferences on giftedness and left-handedness, written numerous articles and books on gifted and dyslexic children, and is the author of the new Ant to Zip series. This is a structured phonic programme for teaching, reading, spelling and handwriting to all children, and especially of use to those with dyslexia/SpLDs.

Mensa

Mensa was founded in England in 1946 and has over 100,000 members from all walks of life worldwide. It is the society for very bright people. Mensa offers people a chance to take a supervised intelligence test; anyone who has a score that puts them in the top 2% (146) is eligible for membership of this world-renowned society. Further details are available from their website.

British Mensa has more than 26,000 members in the UK, including 900 junior Mensans (under 18) – one of these isjust 2.6 years of age (at original time of print).

Organisations that can help the gifted person

There are several organisations that help and support children, parents, teachers and other professional groups. A few of these include:

- Gifted Children's Information Centre.

- National Academy for Gifted and Talented Youth (NAGTY).

- National Association for the Gifted Child.

- The Support Society for Children of High Intelligence (CHI).

- Mensa.

- Pullen Publications (specialises in books for able pupils).

Giftedness checklist

The signs below may indicate whether someone is 'gifted or talented' – they do not need to show all of these signs.

Generally:

- Does not appear to fit in with standard curriculum.

- Has good general knowledge.

- Has a much larger vocabulary than his peer group.

- Has a highly developed verbal aptitude.

- Is interested in many subjects.

- Works well on his own with very limited intervention.

- Will accomplish a variety of things earlier than other children.

- Understands instructions well.
- Concentrates well.
- Is good at problem solving.
- Learns easily and remembers quicker than his peers.
- Will be the best one in his class.
- Will rapidly respond to new ideas.
- Will think of new ways of doing things.
- Is very curious.
- Is very imaginative.
- Generally asks more detailed questions.
- Produces more elaborated answers.
- Is more deeply engaged in testing.
- Is often a group leader.
- Can juggle far more activities and interests than their peer group.
- Has strong opinions.
- Gets on with adults better than his age group.

With mathematics:

- Has a high level of reasoning.
- Understands processes.
- Can complete calculations easily.
- Has a high level of visual spatial ability.

With reading:

- Probably read before he started school.
- Reads a book quickly.

- Has a good ability to decode words.
- Can comprehend complex printed passages.
- Memorises well.

When writing:

- Produces legible print or script.
- Has highly developed ideas.
- Produces very smart written work.

Appears to be very talented in (some not all):

- Music.
- Art.
- Creative writing.
- Scientific thinking.

Summing Up

We should pay particular thanks to people like Dr Peter Congdon who have worked tirelessly to promote giftedness and dyslexia over the last 25 years. It is most important to get these children recognised as early as possible. By identifying a need, you can start to put in the necessary help to support the child. It may be some time before children are routinely screened for giftedness and their needs put into place, but at least we have now made a start.

How Can I Get Help? (10)

What do I do if my child needs help?

If you are concerned that your child is under-achieving at school, you should talk to his teacher. Many parents try to express their concerns with teachers early in the morning, but this can cause problems because mornings are very busy for the teacher who has 30+ children in their classroom. All these children will need some help with coats, buttons, zips, etc. After school is probably best but it can help if you give the teacher a little time to prepare for you.

The fairest way for all concerned would be to explain quickly after school that you are concerned and ask if you could make an appointment in a couple of days time. Not only can the teacher be prepared for it but so can you. Parents tell me they still feel extremely intimidated when they go to the school. I felt the same way for many years – it took me more than 10 years to finally feel at ease. Don't let them make you feel that way! You are a grown-up too!

First things first

It is very important that you keep records of all contact with the school. You can do this simply and easily in a cheap little diary. Every time you speak to anyone at the school (even by telephone) about your child, write down what was said. You will see why this is a valuable exercise later. Don't forget, do it now! You will only forget if you put it off.

The first appointment

Make a list so you can go through it when you see the teacher. Why are you concerned?

- Worried about your child's reading.

- Worried about his spelling.

- What progress is he making compared to other pupils in his class?

- Is he receiving any additional help?

- He doesn't seem to have many friends.

- And so on.

If you are worried about your child then you probably have cause to be – a mother does know best! After you have discussed everything with the teacher, tell him you will monitor the situation and contact him in about a month to see if there is any change in the situation.

Make a diary entry for one month's time. When the time is up, if there has been no significant improvement and you are still concerned about things, contact the teacher again and make another appointment.

The second appointment

Once again, make a list before you go. Work down your list together and explain what progress you have found, if any. If the teacher feels that things are improving and he would like more time, tell him you will monitor the situation for another few weeks. Once again, go home and make a reminder in your diary for a month's time.

The third appointment

If after this time you feel there still has not been any significant improvement and you are still concerned, ask for another appointment. Before you go to the next meeting, write a letter with the points of concern. Ensure you make two copies of this letter.

When you see the teacher, listen to his point of view and exchange ideas. Then if you are still not happy, point out that you have waited over three months for things to improve and you are extremely concerned at your child's lack of progress. Explain that due to the lapse of time you would like the matter looked into officially. Address this letter to the head of the school but give a copy to the teacher and keep a copy in your diary or folder.

Whenever you send a letter to the school or education authority, you should always bear the following in mind:

- Always send your letter in the post or give it to the school secretary.

- Send it Recorded Delivery if you prefer (you pay a little extra for this at the post office).

- If you are sending a copy of the letter to anyone else, it is usual to put the letters CC at the bottom of the page and put the name of the person you are copying the letter to.

- If you are answering a letter from the education authority, always check to see if they have put the initials CC at the end of their letter. If so, you should copy the letter to that person as well.

- When writing always assume the person you are writing to does not know anything about your child; it makes it easier if later on if you have to contact a solicitor.

- Always, always make a copy for your own file and keep it safe.

The letter could be something like this:

Your Name
Your Address
Your Postcode
Your Telephone No.

1st January 2009

Mr A Smith
Head of the School
Anyschool Secondary Modern
Anytown
Wiltshire
SN22 99

Dear Mr Smith

Re: Peter Jones – D.O.B: 1st May 2000

As you are aware, I have been working with you since (look in the diary) concerning Peter's lack of progress.

I am particularly concerned that he is still not able to read, spell and write properly. Peter is becoming more and more withdrawn. Every evening he gets frustrated when attempting to do his homework and then gets very upset. He is lacking in confidence and now has very low self-esteem.

I think that Peter has dyslexia or a specific learning difficulty, therefore, I wish to refer him for a 'Statutory Assessment' under the 1989 Education Act, (Page 42, Code of Practice), so we can get the correct help for him quickly.

I understand you have a time limit of six weeks to indicate that you will or will not make a 'Statutory Assessment'.

I look forward to hearing from you soon.

Yours sincerely

Mr Christopher & Mrs Maria Jones

CC Class Teacher

You can now see why it is vital to keep a list of the dates of every visit to the school and what the outcome of each meeting was. This is extremely important in officially identifying an educational need. These notes will be needed later on.

Once you have given a letter to the teacher (and a copy to the headteacher), you are effectively asking for the first stage of the assessment procedures to be put into place (see chapter 11).

What happens next?

Reports will be compiled from everyone who has dealings with your child to see exactly what the problems are. After looking at all the paperwork from teachers, the education authority and the doctor, the LEA will make a decision as to what help your child needs, if any.

How long does a statutory assessment take?

The 2001 Education Regulations set out time limits for the testing procedures. The process of making a statutory assessment and a statement should take 26 weeks.

In England and Wales, the organisations Network 81 and the BDA have 'befrienders' who can talk you through the Code of Practice and how to succeed. They may be able to go along to meetings with parents. They also have leaflets on getting help for your child with special educational needs.

A more detailed description of the assessment procedure can be found in chapter 11.

SENDIST – Special Educational Needs and Disability Tribunal

The Special Educational Needs and Disability Tribunal (SENDIST) was set up by the Education Act 1993. It is the First Tier Tribunal for Special Educational Needs and Disability. It considers parents' appeals against the decisions of Local Authorities (LAs) about children's special educational needs if parents cannot reach agreement with them. The Tribunal is independent.

Scotland and Northern Ireland – the Code of Practice

The Code of Practice in Scotland and Northern Ireland differs slightly from the England and Wales.

Scotland

The Scottish Parliament passed new legislation under the Additional Support for Learning (Scotland) Act 2004, changing some of the 1984 Act. See below for details:

- Special Educational Needs was replaced by Additional Support Needs.
- Provision is no longer outlined in the Record of Needs.
- The criteria for Additional Support Needs is no longer confined to children with a disability.
- Co-ordinated Support Plans were instituted.
- Requests can be made for all children or young people who have Additional Support Needs.
- New Mediation, Dispute Resolution and Tribunal services were implemented.
- The legal rights of parents, children and young people were altered.

Northern Ireland

The Education (Northern Ireland) Order 1996 amended by the Special Educational Needs and Disability (Northern Ireland) Order 2005 applies. It is similar to England and Wales and states that statutory responsibility for securing provision for special educational needs children lies with the Education and Library Boards and Boards of Governors of mainstream schools.

Summing Up

Speak to your child's teacher as soon as you realise there is a problem. Don't get put off over and over again. Obviously allow the teacher time, but if there is no real progress you must begin formal procedures as soon as you can – ensuring the child's needs are identified and any help is put in place as soon as possible.

Don't worry about the assessment procedures – there are lots of people who can help you through this difficult time.

How to Obtain Help for Your Child's Special Educational Needs (11)

By Dr D Cowell B.Sc. M.Phil. Ph.D. Dip. Psych.

The most important law dealing with special educational needs is the 1996 Education Act. This act is explained in the Special Educational Needs Code of Practice. An updated version was published in 2001. The Code of Practice gives practical guidance on how to identify and assess children with special educational needs.

All early education provision, Local Authority Schools and Local Education Authorities must take account of this code when they are dealing with children who have, or might have, special educational needs. Professional reports must take account of the Code of Practice and provide the required detailed information.

Health and social services must also take account of the code when helping Local Education Authorities.

The basic principles of the Code of Practice are as follows:

- All children with special educational needs should have those needs met.

- Most children with special educational needs will have those needs met in ordinary schools.

- The views of parents must be taken into account at all times.

- Children with special educational needs should receive a broad, well- balanced education which, as far as possible, is based upon the National Curriculum.

- The wishes of the child should, as far as possible, be taken into account.

The term special educational needs has a legal definition. Children with special educational needs all have learning difficulties or disabilities that make it more difficult for them to learn than most other children of the same age.

The law says that children do not have learning difficulties just because their first language is not English. Of course, some of these children may have learning difficulties as well.

Approximately 20% of children will have special educational needs of some kind at some time during their education. A few children, approximately 2%, will need substantial extra help for all their time in school.

Here are some examples of special educational needs. A child has difficulties with:

■ All the work undertaken in school.

■ Some activities: reading, writing, number work, remembering information.

■ Expressing themselves or understanding what others are saying.

■ Making friends and getting on well with adults.

■ Physical or sensory difficulties.

■ Behaving properly in school.

■ Organising themselves.

■ Some kind of sensory difficulty, for example with hearing or eyesight.

■ Some physical difficulty which may affect their learning or adjustment to school.

The Special Educational Needs Code of Practice provides the framework for action. Schools are required to have their own special educational needs policy. They are also required to have a person in charge of special needs. Such a person is normally called the special educational needs co-ordinator or SENCO. The school is required to follow a graduated approach. This means that they have to set up a step-by-step plan to resolve, or clarify, the exact nature of the child's difficulties.

The school must inform the parents when they start to give extra or different help for the child. In early education, this help is called Early Years Action. In normal schools, this help is called School Action. If the child does not make sufficient progress, the class teacher or the SENCO will then talk to the parents about obtaining advice from other specialists outside the school. They might want to ask for help from, for example, a specialist teacher, an educational psychologist, a speech and language therapist or another help professional. This kind of help is called Early Years Action Plus or, in the case of schools, School Action Plus.

The SENCO will include the parent in discussions and will consider parental views in making decisions. SENCOs should keep parents fully informed about the child's progress.

At the stage of School Action or School Action Plus, the child will normally have an Individual Education Plan (IEP).

The IEP should say:

- What special help is being given.

- How often the child will receive help.

- Who will provide the help.

- What the targets for your child are.

- How and when your child's progress will be checked.

- What help you can give your child at home.

As a parent, you can approach your child's teacher or the SENCO at any time. In some areas there is a Parent Partnership Service that can give the names of local voluntary organisations and parents' groups which might be able to help.

Sometimes the School Action and School Action Plus does not succeed in fully resolving the child's difficulties. Such children, who have long-term and specialist requirements, will be considered for a Statement of Special Educational Needs. This is normally described as a statement. This statement describes all the child's needs and all the special help that he or she requires. Approximately 2% of children will enter special schools or units.

Children who require long-term special help normally have a statutory assessment. This is a detailed investigation to find out exactly what your child's special needs are and what special help the child needs. A statutory assessment is only required if the school or early education setting cannot provide all the help that your child requires.

Your child's school or early education setting can ask the Local Education Authority to carry out a statutory assessment. They will always talk to you before asking the LEA.

Similarly, you can ask the LEA yourself to carry out the statutory assessment. However, you should always talk to your child's teachers or the SENCO before asking the LEA.

If the LEA decides not to assess your child, you can appeal to the Special Educational Needs Tribunal to ask them to change the LEA's decision. Alternatively, if the LEA wish to carry out the statutory assessment and you do not agree with this, you can go to the tribunal in the same way.

If the LEA carries out a statutory assessment, they will ask a number of professionals employed in the public sector to give their views on your child. The LEA will ask for advice from:

■ The teachers in your child's school or early education setting.

■ An educational psychologist.

- A qualified medical practitioner.

- Social services (who will only give advice if they know your child).

- Anyone else whose advice the LEA considers appropriate.

Parents have the right to be present at any interview, medical or other test during the statutory assessment. Sometimes the professionals may ask to see the child without the parents as children sometimes behave differently when parents are present.

Parents should provide a written record of their views as part of the statutory assessment. Parents can also send the LEA any private advice or opinions that they have obtained. The LEA will take these into account as part of the assessment.

As part of the assessment process, the LEA will send parents details of schools which are suitable for children with special educational needs.

Parents have a right to say which Local Authority School they wish their child to attend, either mainstream or special. The LEA must agree with the parents' preference as long as:

- The school you choose is suitable for your child's age, ability and special educational needs.

- Your child's attendance will not hinder the education of other children already at the school.

- Placing your child in the school will represent an efficient use of the LEA's resources.

You may wish your child to go to a school which is not run by an LEA. This could be a non-maintained special school or an independent school that you feel can meet your child's needs. The LEA will consider your wishes carefully before they make a final decision, but if there is a suitable state school, the LEA have no legal duty to spend public money on a place for your child at a non-maintained or independent school.

After the statutory assessment, the LEA may decide to draw up a Statement of Special Educational Needs. If you disagree with what is in the statement, you should first ask the named officer of the LEA for an explanation. If you are still not happy, you have the right to appeal to the Special Educational Needs Tribunal with reference to:

- Part 2 – the description of your child's special educational needs.

- Part 3 – the help to be given to your child to meet those needs.

- Part 4 – the type and name of the school which the LEA thinks your child should attend.

The LEA will tell parents about the local arrangements for resolving disagreements. This is normally the appropriate course of action before appealing to the SEN Tribunal.

The LEA must keep your child's progress under review and ensure that the statement continues to meet their special educational needs. The review of the statement must occur at least once a year but LEAs can review it more often if necessary.

If your child has a Statement of Special Educational Needs, the Annual Review in Year 9 is particularly important in preparing for their move to further education, higher education and adult life. The review will discuss a Transition Plan for your child's move to adult life.

Education for young people with special educational needs does not stop at 16+. Depending on their abilities and requirements, they can stay at an ordinary or special school, or can move to a college of further education or into work-based training. Children who leave school to attend further education will not normally keep the statement. However, the college will continue to monitor their progress and give appropriate help.

The SEN Tribunal only deals with a limited number of situations, as described above. However, if your complaint is about something else, you may be able to take matters to the local government Ombudsman. An example of this would be if the LEA did not keep within the required time limits.

The Department for Education and Skills (now called Department for Children, Schools and Families) produces a guide for parents and carers entitled Special Educational Needs (SEN). In this publication, the important point is made (page 3) that parents may wish to talk to someone who is independent and knows about special educational needs.

The booklet goes on to say that you can get help from the local Parent Partnership Service or from national or local voluntary organisations, which are mainly charities.

One reason for obtaining independent advice is that the person you see may be able to be more objective than somebody who is, for example, employed by the LEA with whom you are negotiating.

Another advantage is that you can seek help from a person of your own choice. For example, you could refer to your own psychologist or medical practitioner. Many private practitioners have long experience in specialised areas of special educational needs. They will usually have substantial experience in either the Health Service or Local Education Authorities, or both.

Private practitioners will normally subscribe to a code of practice laid down by their professional body. They are also likely to have their own professional indemnity insurance.

A further advantage is that the private practitioner would be available to you if the child moves to a new school or if you move to a new area. Within LEA or National Health Service settings, such moves usually involve a complete change of the professional personnel who have been involved with your child.

Families who have private health insurance can sometimes obtain the help of a private practitioner through the insurance scheme. In such cases, the Special Educational Needs booklet makes it clear (page 16) that private advice must be taken into account as part of the assessment by the LEA.

Two names and addresses are particularly important for parents to know about. Firstly, the Special Educational Needs Tribunal provides a special booklet which can be obtained from the LEA or from the SEN Tribunal. You can find out more about the local government Ombudsman in a special booklet, obtainable from the LEA or from the Ombudsman's office.

Scotland and Northern Ireland

Scotland and Northern Ireland have a separate Code of Practice. For further details of the Code of Practice, please see chapter 10.

The Role of the Psychiatrist (12)

By Dr R Eyre

Consultant in Child and Adolescent Psychiatry

Introduction

Every district has its own Child and Adolescent Mental Health Services. These may be found within a hospital setting or in a community-based clinic. They also may carry different service titles, e.g. Child Guidance, Child and Family Consultation, Child Psychiatry. In the past, such clinics were often run in partnership with education and social services, but nowadays they tend to be NHS resources. Referrals are accepted from all professionals working with children and often from parents themselves.

Only in a minority of cases do children have mental illnesses seen in the adult population. The majority of children will have emotional or behavioural difficulties that they and their families can see are causing them problems in their normal social or educational progress. There will often be stressful factors in the background contributing to the presenting problem. These could include family break-up or relationship problems, bereavements, chronic physical illness and school difficulties. The Child and Adolescent Mental Health Services have a range of professionals who may be able to offer help, including psychiatrists, clinical psychologists, family therapists, community nurses, psychotherapists and specialist teachers. All these people will have regular links with schools and nurseries and the local authority.

Special learning difficulties

Dyslexia is certainly one problem that may cause stress and distress in a child, leading to possible emotional and behaviour difficulties if it is not detected and appropriately managed in school. Most child psychiatrists prefer to use the term specific learning difficulties rather than dyslexia.

A child has a specific learning difficulty when his or her performance on a certain learning task (reading, spelling, numerical skills) falls 28 months behind that which would be usual for that child's age and overall ability. It can lead to many difficulties in the classroom setting. Often such children have good oral verbal abilities, so it can be confusing and upsetting for them not to be able to translate this ability into their reading, writing or spelling skills. It can also be confusing for class teachers who may see a child as underachieving or unmotivated rather than having a specific problem.

It is not difficult to see that children will often feel bad about their difficulty and may seek to avoid it by distracting behaviour away from the educational activity. They may develop a low self-esteem and become anxious about school. They may be seen as misbehaving or disruptive in class when they avoid the work that is difficult. If the problem is not recognised, the child can move on to becoming a child with behavioural difficulties.

Research shows us that children with specific learning difficulties are more likely to develop later conduct disorders than children without those problems. It is, however, not an inevitable progression since it is more the maladaptive responses of the child and others to the learning difficulties that lead to a poor outcome rather than the learning difficulties per se.

Specific learning difficulties may be associated with other problems too. Poor coordination, difficulties with concentration and over activity are more often seen in children with these difficulties than on average.

Management issues in specific learning difficulties

The Child Mental Health Services can be helpful in:

- Addressing secondary behaviour difficulties.

- Assessing over activity and poor concentration.

- Detecting or diagnosing specific learning difficulties in the above as a presenting problem.

- Advising other professionals and agencies.

Psychological testing is always necessary to diagnose specific learning difficulties, and ordinarily an educational psychologist would do this. Sometimes, however, the clinical psychologist with Child and Adolescent Mental Health Services can also contribute to the assessment.

Once the diagnosis has been made, the most important next step is that parents and professionals alike are aware of the specific areas of difficulty that the child has. The Education Department will then make special needs provision for the extra teaching input necessary, and it is helpful for parents to have regular communication set up with their child's teachers. Sometimes extra tuition from specialist teachers outside of school may be helpful, so long as there is good communication between school and tutor.

Acknowledgment of the problem and appropriate educational measures can go a long way towards improving concerns over a child's difficult behaviour or low self-esteem. Sometimes the child and their family need ongoing support and help with these issues, and this is where Child and Adolescent Mental Health Services can continue to help after the diagnosis has been made.

Computers and Dyslexia/SpLDs (13)

During the last decade there have been tremendous strides in the field of technology. There is such a vast array of specialist software for people with learning difficulties of any type that I can only provide an overview of the types available.

Can computers help with dyslexic students?

Computers are now an important part of classroom teaching. Although no computer package can ever be a substitute for good teaching, the correct software packages can help and support the busy teacher. Many programs can be incorporated into a specialist-teaching scheme. They provide over learning, structured and systematic teaching, immediate reinforcement and feedback, and the additional motivation that students require to succeed.

The advantage of instant feedback and the possibility of echoing each letter name, each word, each sentence of any marked section of text, as well as reading through, helps the student with poor short-term memory and ensures an efficient transfer to long-term memory – making learning fun. Software packages can provide structured learning, continually developing skills and providing support for literacy and numeracy.

How can computers help learners?

Computers can help people with learning difficulties in lots of different ways:

- Learning to use databases and spreadsheets may aid sequential thinking and problem solving skills.

- They can motivate people, especially children.

- There is immediate reinforcement.

- Students have the ability to make and self-correct mistakes in private.

- They provide essential over learning/reinforcement.

- Most computers can now be programmed to 'speak to you'. This software could revolutionise foreign language learning. Programs with speech make learning truly multi-sensory.

- Students can listen – ideas developed orally can be tried out and changed easily.

- Response is immediate.

- Students work at own pace.

- Printouts and text on a screen are often easier to read than the student's own writing.

- Reading and spelling are incorporated into nearly every program.

- The colours and brightness on computer screens can be adjusted.

Computer equipment – hardware

The first three items are the bare minimum when using computers. The remaining items are useful. What hardware the student needs will depend on their individual difficulty.

1. Laptop computer.

2. Internet and email.

3. Printer with built in scanner, if possible.

4. Portable USB memory sticks.

5. Electronic gadgets.

Specialist computers or keyboards

6. Keyboard – ideal for people with disabilities.

7. Touch screen computers – also ideal for people with disabilities.

8. Hands free computers – also ideal for people with disabilities.

1. Laptop computers

Laptops are the most popular computers these days because of their size. They can range from just £399. Most computers in this range incorporate speakers and sound cards (i.e. multimedia) that make it ideal for specialist educational software.

2. Internet and email

The internet is invaluable for research and emails. If you do not have it at home, almost all schools, colleges and libraries allow free access.

3. Printer

There is a vast array of printers on offer. Many printers now incorporate scanners so you do not have to have a separate one.

4. Portable USB memory sticks

A Portable USB Memory Stick CD 4GB costs about £5.00 and is an excellent investment as you can download data and transfer it to other computers. Information can be downloaded quickly onto a small stick (which looks like a pen).

5. Electronic gadgets

There is a wide range of electronic gadgets available today, specifically for the dyslexic user. You will find a large selection of them from a company called iANSYST.

6. Keyboards – for nursery/Key Stage 1 children or children with dyspraxia)

BigKeys is a starter keyboard and has a lower-case keyboard. It has been designed for nursery/Key Stage 1 children and it has a colourful and uncluttered layout in the traditional 'qwerty' style. All unnecessary keys are removed or hidden. The very large keys are colour coded – vowels are yellow, 'r' is red, 'b' is blue, etc – further aiding letter recognition. This beginner's keyboard makes an excellent start before changing to the standard keyboard. It is very easy to use; no software needed – just plug in and go. An excellent choice for very young children. Further information from KeyTools.

7. Touch screen computers

These computers look like any other monitor but they work by simply touching the screen with your hands. They are very useful in identifying and assessing children (of three years plus) for early signs of specific learning difficulties. These can be bought quite cheaply – the Edge10 TS700 17 inch UXGA Multimedia Touch Screen LCD Monitor is just £245.

8. The hands-free computer

Hands-free computers use neither screen, keyboard or mouse. Hand movements control them in mid-air. The 'virtual computer' is used in some offices and operating theatres. Hand movements in mid-air are picked up by cameras coupled to pattern recognition software and used to control the computer in the same way as a mouse does. These systems cost more than conventional computers. However, their use for people with disabilities is infinite.

Software

There are probably thousands of software packages available now. I have only included a few of the most tried and tested ones which support reading, spelling, numeracy, writing skills and organisational and planning skills.

1. Word processor, spreadsheets and database.

2. Speech recognition.

3. Word prediction and speech synthesis.

4. Reading and spelling.

5. Punctuation.

6. Grammar.

7. Handwriting.

8. Maths.

9. Mind mapping.

10. Study skills.

11. Speech training.

12. Games.

1.Word processor, spreadsheets and database

A word processor is the most important piece of software required. People with learning difficulties are finding that when they use a word processor, 'the written world opens up' to them. Most good word processors incorporate a spell checker and a grammar checker.

I prefer to use Microsoft Office XP software – this is very simple to use and has a good spell checker and grammar checker included. It also has spreadsheets, database and speech recognition built in (see below). Many offices use this software. Most schools allow students to use computers to complete GCSE coursework and some examinations.

2. Speech recognition software (SR or SRs)

During the last few years, speech recognition software has come a very long way. Some of these software packages are now rated independently to be 97% accurate. If you are buying a new computer, make sure it is a certified 'speech recognition ready machine'.

This software works by 'talking' to your computer. As you talk, the words are written on the computer screen – and they are spelt correctly. This type of software helps to improve spelling because the student always sees the correctly spelled words. The computer types up exactly what you say. The golden rule is to speak slowly when recording your own voice, stressing 'a', 'an', 'and', etc.

Office XP now has voice recognition software built-in. However, if a student has dyslexia or dysgraphia, in my opinion they would find it easier to use separate voice recognition software, such as the one below.

Dragon Naturally Speaking 10

This easy to use speech solution allows you to create, edit and revise documents without using a keyboard. This software is one of my favourites and in my opinion, is one of the best on the market for dyslexic students. You can get further information from REM.

3. Word prediction and speech synthesis

Word prediction and speech synthesis software 'predicts' what the student wants to say by 'guessing' what the word is from the first couple of letters. With some of these packages the computer will search the list for the appropriate word, i.e. type the letter 'a' and several of the common words are suggested such as a, an, and, another, etc. The user can normally listen to the words being spoken thus helping them decide which word is correct.

ClaroRead Plus

The ClaroRead Plus is a word prediction program which includes ScreenRuler (a strip-magnifying program), the new ClaroView screen tinting program and Scan2Text which uses the powerful OmniPage optical character recognition for turning paper and PDF files into editable, speaking Word documents.

Penfriend XP

Able to predict words before they are typed, saving time and effort. It can also speak its suggestions and read text from documents. A great help for those with dyslexia. It has been so successful it has been sold to all schools in Northern Ireland as well as all UK online centres in colleges and libraries (nearly 900 centres). You can get further information from Penfriend.

Penfriend XP - Portable

As above but is portable. It's ideal to take from classroom to classroom or office to home. You can get further information from REM.

Read and Write Gold

Providing the ultimate support for dyslexic students and adults, this toolbar offers a variety of tools. Combinations of speech-feedback, phonetic spellchecker and dictionary and word predictions help overcome the problems of accessing and composing written material. It can correct words such as 'there', 'they're', and 'their' where the sound of the word is correct but the context may be wrong. You can get further information from iANSYST.

4. Reading and spelling

Wordshark 3 (5 – 14)

This is one of the best reading and spelling software packages. Based on Alpha to Omega by Dr Beve Hornsby and Frula Shear, it is used in hundreds of establishments across the country. There are hundreds of word lists with lots of games to help reading and spelling. The lists include the National Literacy Strategy high frequency words and you can also add your own word lists. Designed for Key Stages 1 to 3. Available from iANSYST.

Units of sound (9 – adult)

This multi-sensory reading intervention program also develops spelling skills. The structured, cumulative program builds reading accuracy, vocabulary, sentence writing, spelling comprehension and listening skills. It includes a screening test to ensure placement at the correct level. Available from LDA.

Nessy (5 – adult)

This is a complete interactive literacy teaching program consisting of 14 sections, each containing reading and spelling checks. Available from iANSYST.

GAMZ Player CD (7 – adult)

This is based on the popular GAMZ card games. It has many additional features and activities to support reading, phonics and spelling. Available from iANSYST.

5. Punctuation

The Punctuation Show

An excellent package for teaching the rules of punctuation. Many activities explain and then go over basic skills. Areas covered include apostrophes, brackets, hyphens, dashes, capital letters, full stops, commas, semicolons, colons, speech marks, question marks and exclamation marks. Available from Dyslexic.com.

Penfriend XL

New in 2004. Information as above but works with mostly European languages.

textHELP

Providing the ultimate support for dyslexic students and adults, this toolbar offers a variety of tools. Combinations of speech-feedback, phonetic spell checker and dictionary and word predictions help overcome the problems of accessing and composing written material. You can get further information from iANSYST.

6. Grammar

The Grammar Show (7 – 14)

This helps children learn and consolidate their understanding of grammar. Suitable for Key Stage 2 and 3. Areas covered: nouns, simple verbs and tenses, verb forms, adjectives and adverbs, pronouns and prepositions, sentences and standard English. Available from www.dyslexic.com.

7. Handwriting

Claude and Maude is a useful handwriting software package. It is ideal for students with dysgraphia or handwriting problems. It helps reinforce the knowledge needed to form each letter. You can also print out worksheets in any size enabling younger children to work at their own pace/style. This is available from SEMERC.

8. Maths

Numbershark (5 – 16)

One of the best maths packages but needs some adult supervision for programming. The structured learning task covers the four main rules of number, addition, subtraction, multiplication and division. Available from NFER NELSON.

Key Stage Maths Invaders (all ages)

An excellent package to practise basic number skills by playing 'space invaders'. Available from iANSYST.

9. Mind mapping

Some dyslexics prefer a visual working environment. Mind-mapping software makes it easy to get ideas down and then rearrange them into order. They can be used to brainstorm, write essays, revise projects, take notes, etc.

Inspiration v8 (7 – adult)

An excellent visual learning tool. A great computer program that maps out ideas in a nifty spider chart. Helps students develop ideas while planning and structuring workflow. Available from iANSYST.

10. Study skills

Technology has made studying so much easier for all students – not just dyslexic ones. Many programs can help with time management, planning, note taking, reading and writing.

WordsWork

This programme is written primarily for dyslexic adults. It uses a multi-sensory approach for helping the older dyslexic student improve their study skills. WordsWork has very good graphics and uses humour to encourage students to develop a variety of language skills. Using a "learning style" approach, students are encouraged to identify and use their strengths to overcome areas of weakness. Available from iANSYST.

11. Speech training

Computers are now helping children at some schools to learn to speak properly. A speech training aid computer displays the word it wants a child to say and listens to the way the child repeats the word. It then tells them if they have said it correctly. Once the child has said the word correctly, he can move on to the next word.

There are thousands of words with graphics available. Teachers using the software are impressed at the computer's ability to 'hear' them talking. The Defence Research Agency and Hereford and Worcester County Council initially developed the project jointly.

12. Games

I am including games in this section because many parents often see arcade type games as children just playing. But playing these games can help develop hand/eye coordination, and a fun approach is adopted to make learning almost painless. Sinking battleships in alphabetical order is far more exciting than looking for X, Y, Z, etc on a keyboard!

Accessories

1. Portable dictionaries and spell checkers.

2. Recording equipment.

3. PDAs – Personal Digital Assistants.

4. Quicktionary Reading Pen II.

5. Portable word processors.

1. Portable dictionaries and spell checkers

Franklin UK English dictionary/thesaurus (11 – adult)

This pocket sized Collins UK dictionary, thesaurus and phonetic spell checker weighs less than 100g. It contains a comprehensive dictionary and thesaurus. Features include LCD screen, word games and ROM card slot. It is the ideal portable solution for dyslexic students. Available from iANYST.

PageMark electronic dictionary

This is absolutely superb; it is called Page Mark because that is exactly how thin it is. You can slide it into any book you are reading, and it is always at hand to help you.

It includes over 145,000 words, phrases and definitions from the Compact Oxford English Dictionary and automatic spelling correction.

Franklin Literacy Word Bank (5 – 11)

Designed to support the National Curriculum and National Literacy Scheme. Includes a portable dictionary, thesaurus and spell checker. Perfect for young children in Key Stage 1 and 2. Available from iANYST.

2. Recording equipment

Digital voice recorder (11 – adult)

Several of these are available, including the Olympus VN-1200 Digital Voice Recorder. An easy-to-use, small device, with a powerful memory (64mb). This is an excellent recorder for note taking and dictation and can be linked directly to the computer.

Micro cassette recorder (7 – adult)

Lots of these are now on the market; they are very small and compact, and are excellent for taking notes in the classroom. The Sony M800V is an excellent choice, ultra slim with good sound quality and extremely small compared to a normal tape recorder.

3. PDAs (Personal Digital Assistants)

PDAs give you one big advantage over any other small computer – you can view and edit data while away from your main computer. They are very useful for people with dyslexia and short-term memory difficulties. Most of them have the ability to set reminders for appointments, create 'to-do' lists and read and edit documents. There are two main operating systems: Windows Pocket PC2000 and the Palm operating systems. Both allow you to synchronise your documents with Windows applications on your home computer.

Palm Tungsten C (PDA) (14 – adult)

View and edit MS Office documents on the move and keep track of appointments and tasks using the software provided. Available from iANYST.

Palm Zire 71 (11 – adult)

Get organised with the Palm. Synchronise appointments and contacts with your PC ideas and notes on screen. Available from iANYST.

4. Quicktionary Reading Pen 11, Oxford edition (11 – adult)

This portable reading pen has been designed specifically for people with dyslexia. It literally 'reads' words aloud and is just a little bigger than a normal pen. Glide the pen over a word, see it on the display and then hear it read and spelt out loud – it will even give pronunciations. It has been used successfully in schools, colleges, libraries and resource centres.

5. Portable word processors

AlphaSmart Neo (5 – adult)

A popular, inexpensive battery-powered word processor with easy, one-key transfer to PC for formatting. This high-powered keyboard is a must for writers and students at all levels. Available from REM.

AlphaSmart Dana

A true alternative to the laptop computer. It has a full sized keyboard and brings Palm technology to dyslexic and dyspraxic students. This is very useful for word processing, spreadsheets and organisational applications. It comes with spell checkers, a thesaurus, calendar, address book and calculator. It is very lightweight and has a long battery life of 25 hours. This is a cheap portable writing aid and very robust for children's bags. Available from REM.

Agents for software

Here are just a few of the companies that sell software:

■ REM.

■ iANSYST.

■ Dyslexia Computer Resource Centre.

■ AVP.

- Dyslexia Educational Resources.

Computers in examinations

Special arrangements

The Examination Board Regulations for Special Arrangements state that these arrangements are made to enable candidates with a disability (e.g. dyslexia/SpLDs) to show their attainment when otherwise they might not be able to do so. (Special arrangements should not give an advantage over other candidates.)

Each examination board is different. The school has to check in advance with the relevant board to ascertain exactly what the student can use. This must be done in good time.

Any special arrangements must have been recommended by an educational psychologist and the report must state the exact nature of the special arrangement required. However, in order to free up time with educational psychologists, some specialist teachers, who have additional training, can now arrange for a reader, extra time, etc.

Some special arrangements can include:

- Use of a word processor (spell checkers to be turned off).
- Use of typewriter.
- Use of speech recognition software in examinations.
- Extra time.

The British Dyslexic Computer Committee

The British Dyslexic Computer Committee has been reviewing programs for dyslexia for many years. There are a series of booklets which are updated frequently. For further information, contact the BDA.

Summing Up

Computers are a great help in education. Over the last few years, in relative terms, they have become cheaper, making them more accessible for the average family. Specialist software has also greatly improved and become a lot cheaper. You can get software to help you learn a language, play the piano or even learn to cook.

A lot of dyslexic people say when they use a computer, 'the written world opens up to them'.

Selecting a School and Private Tuition (14)

It is very difficult for anyone to advise on the type of school you should be looking for as every child's needs are so different. The majority of children will simply go to the school in their immediate vicinity, but specialist schooling is slightly different because there is not usually a lot of choice. It is best to speak to as many people as you can, including teachers, the education authority's advisors and other parents – the decision is then up to you.

It is important that the correct school is identified for your child. Sometimes, although a school is on your doorstep, it may not always be the best one for your child's special needs. Visit all the schools in your area and see what specialist provision they can offer.

There are many different types of schools. These are just a few:

■ Mainstream schools (your local school).

■ The independent sector.

■ Dyslexia schools.

■ Schools for deaf children.

■ Schools for blind children.

State schools – mainstream

The majority of schools in the country are operated by the government/LEAs. Most of these are ordinary mainstream schools.

Even if children have special needs, i.e., dyslexia, dyspraxia, etc, the child usually stays in mainstream schooling. This is usually considered best for the child and the family. It is only in extreme cases (if the school cannot meet the needs of the individual child) that they would go to a specialist school. Some mainstream schools have units attached to them for dyslexia, etc, or therapists and other specialists can come into the school on a regular basis.

A booklet is available from your LEA with a list of all schools in your area.

Independent schools

There are two main bodies that deal with the independent sector: CReSTeD and the Independent Schools Council (ISC).

CReSTeD

This is the Council for the Registration of Schools Teaching Dyslexic Pupils, and it maintains a list of schools that meet CReSTeD criteria.

The Independent Schools Council

The Independent Schools Council has a comprehensive list of the majority of schools in the independent sector. It has details of all schools on its register and in what the school specialises in (if anything).

The ISC represent approximately 1300 independent (or private) schools in the UK. These schools charge parents to send their children to them. There is sometimes help available towards the school fees. Some private schools are boarding and others are day schools.

Grants

It is very difficult to obtain a grant for dyslexia as there are always so many applicants chasing a very small pot. However, there are several organisations which may be able to help and reference books are usually available in the library. One book that deals solely with grants is The Educational Grants Directory.

Dyslexia schools

The majority of schools that specialise in dyslexia are private (at the moment, I think there are just a couple in the state sector). Some of these schools are just for dyslexic pupils; the others have dyslexic units attached to them.

These schools are usually the best place for children with severe dyslexia. Children who attend these schools enjoy themselves because they are 'the same' as everyone else. The majority of these schools take students for a period of time (approximately two years) and then the children go back into mainstream schooling.

There are specialist schools for SpLDs/dyslexia which are approved by the Independent Schools Joint Council and the Council for the Registration of Schools.

The Portage Service

The Portage Service (National Portage Association) is a home visiting educational service for pre-school children with additional support needs and their families. It aims to support the development of young children's play, communication and relationships and to encourage full participation in day-to-day life within the family and beyond the home. Ask your health visitor for more information or look at the Portage website: www.portage.org.uk.

Pupil Referral Units (PRU)

Pupil Referral Units (PRUs) provide education to children who, because of illness, exclusion, or other reason, do not/cannot attend mainstream schooling. Children usually attend a PRU for a fixed period of time and then return to mainstream school.

Blind/deaf schools

Many charities including the RNIB and the RNID have several specialist schools. They also give help, guidance and training to mainstream schools so the majority of children can stay in their local schools.

Other schools

This covers a very wide area of specialist schools including art, science, drama, behaviour, handicapped, dyspraxic and many others.

Education centres

If your child is struggling at school then private tuition can make all the difference. There are quite a few private education centres around the country that operate between 9.00am to 5.00pm, Monday to Friday and Saturday mornings. These centres have thousands of pounds for specialist teaching and testing equipment. Children usually work for one-hour sessions.

The school can make an 'approved absence' for an education activity. The children usually come out of school for an hour once or twice each week. Most schools are quite happy for this – the children may miss a little time at school but it means they are not tired at the end of the day and so can progress rapidly. I personally do not think we should expect children to do extra work after school each day (on top of their usual homework). My own children would certainly have kicked up about it!

The fees for these centres are usually approximately £30 – £50 per hour.

Private tutors

There are many private tutors who work from home in the evening. They usually charge approximately £15 – £25 per hour. Lessons take place after school. Word of mouth is the best recommendation but please make sure the teachers:

- are suitably qualified with an SpLD qualification.

- regularly update their knowledge with suitable courses.

- have references available and that you see them.

- have certificates confirming police checks (from the Criminal Records Bureau or CRB) and that you ask to see them.

When teaching, does the teacher:

- use a multi-sensory programme such as Hickey, Alpha to Omega, etc?

- Ffeel qualified to undertake further assessments as necessary?

- have computer software to reinforce what the child has learnt and to stop the child from being bored?

- follow the recommendations from any psychologist's/school report?

- liase with the school as necessary?

- give homework each week?

- assess/test at regular intervals?

- give out regular progress reports, and do they charge extra for them?

Checklist for selecting a school

Selecting a school for your child is not always easy. The school nearest to you may not be the best one to help your child.

Below is an example of what your checklist for selecting a school should include.

General

- Ask the school for a prospectus.
- Visit the school on a normal working day.
- Find out if the school has a home/school contract.
- What does the school do about discipline issues?
- Does the school have an anti-bullying policy?
- Try to meet all teachers who will come into contact with your child, especially the special needs staff.

Specialist teaching unit – staff

- How many special needs staff are employed at the school?
- What qualifications do they have?
- Does the school provide in-house training for SpLD teachers?
- Do teachers keep up-to-date with special needs courses?
- How many times do other professionals such as psychologists and speech therapists (if applicable to your case) come into the school?
- Do dyslexic children have to take foreign languages?

Specialist teaching unit – students

If your child has specialist tuition:

- How many hours is it for each week?

- How is it arranged?

- Are the lessons carried out individually or in a group? How many are in a group?

- When are these lessons held? (It is important that it is not during your child's favourite subject.)

- Who takes these lessons and what are their qualifications? (Sometimes schools use 'helpers' with no experience at all.)

- How often do they monitor progress?

- When do they call in the appropriate specialist help, i.e., psychologist, etc?

- How are details of the child's learning difficulties passed on to other non- specialist staff?

- Are you kept up-to-date with the progress or concerns?

Specialist equipment – general

- Does the school use special equipment, i.e., computers, tape recorders, voice recognition software, etc?

- Does the school use specialist software (recommended by the BDA)?

- Will students with special needs be able to use laptops, computers, notebooks, palm held organisers, PDAs, etc, for their coursework?

Dyslexia-friendly schools pack

The 4th edition of the updated resource pack is free and available to primary and secondary schools. It has information, tips and ideas on how to make school dyslexia friendly.

The pack is available via the BDA website or from REM (see help list for contact details).

Summing Up

It is important that the correct school is identified for your child. Although a school is on your doorstep, it may not always be the best one for your child's special needs. Visit all the schools in your area and see what specialist provision they can offer.

There are many private centres around which can provide access to extra tuition on a regular weekly basis. You may like to supplement your child's education with this or with private tutors. Both can help tremendously.

Health Problems (15)

There are many medical reasons for students failing at school. The most obvious is if they cannot see or hear properly as they will not be able to read/write or respond appropriately. If you suspect your child may have a problem, this should be checked immediately. Your doctor or health visitor will be able to arrange for a medical or hearing test. Your local optometrists will carry out a full eye test, even with very young children.

There are many health problems that could affect your child at school. A few are listed below.

1. General poor health.

2. Deafness.

3. Temporary deafness (glue ear).

4. Sight-loss.

5. Light sensitivity.

6. Lack of vitamins (see chapter 18).

Arranging a medical

If the school is concerned that your child is not performing as well as he should be, they will ask for an Assessment of Educational Needs; part of the assessment will include a medical. The medical is usually carried out in your own home so you can express any concerns you have with the doctor.

Deafness in children

There are about nine million people with a permanent hearing loss in the UK; approximately 25,000 of these are children. Many more experience temporary hearing problems in early childhood.

Deafness is often associated with older people but many children are born deaf or profoundly deaf – others become so after an illness. One million children (0 to eight years) will experience temporary deafness caused by glue ear.

Checking your child's hearing – the Newborn Hearing Screening Programme

In the UK, the Newborn Hearing Screening Programme started in 2005 and most children born after that date will have had their hearing checked at birth. If you think there may still be a problem you can ask your health visitor to arrange for further testing to be carried out. Some schools employ a school nurse so child's hearing will be routinely checked once they starts school.

Pardon! What did you say?

If your child cannot hear properly, it may be causing his problems. However, there may be a simple remedy that can correct the problem almost immediately. Wax in the ear canal is the most common problem.

Wax is made normally but becomes a problem if excessive amounts are produced. It forms into small beads, mixes with dust and dead skin and falls out of the ear. This cleaning mechanism works well for most people and does not need any additional help, e.g., with cotton tipped sticks or fingers, etc.

However, some people make abnormal amounts of wax and may have to have it removed by a doctor or nurse.

Glue ear

This is a common condition in childhood. The tube becomes obstructed by adenoids at the back of the nose so air cannot enter the middle ear and the cavity fills with fluid. The eardrum becomes dark looking and, as time goes on, the fluid becomes thicker until it has the consistency of thick glue. Often the only sign is deafness. Children's schooling may suffer and behaviour may deteriorate.

In a lot of cases it will clear by itself, but in severe cases treatment will involve making a small hole in the drum, usually under a general anaesthetic. A tube (grommet) may be inserted and the adenoids may be removed. Adenoids usually disappear at puberty and most children with glue ear do not need treatment after this time. The hearing is usually restored to normal.

Where can I get help?

The RNID (Royal National Institute for Deaf People) is the largest charity representing the nine million both deaf and hard of hearing people in the UK. It campaigns for improvements in facilities and services, and for more awareness of deafness by both government bodies and members of the public. It also campaigns in particular for integrated schooling (where applicable) and encourages greater public awareness of these problems.

Do deaf children have to attend a special school?

A large percentage of deaf children attend ordinary mainstream schools. Many of them receive additional special education support within their schools.

Sight problems

Visual problems are one of the most common causes of disability in the world. In Britain around two million people have sight problems – approximately 24,000 of these are children.

Most parents visit their doctor and dentist regularly, yet many of them still do not appreciate the importance of taking their children to the optometrists. (Until recently we called them opticians.)

The Optical Information Council has estimated that one child in five may have undetected visual problems yet half of all parents with children under eight have never taken their children for an eye test. Regular eye tests, using new techniques, may prevent children with learning difficulties from being labelled problem children and would enable them to be identified at a much earlier age. It is imperative that these tests are carried out before the child starts to fail as the damage caused to their self-esteem is very difficult to restore.

Your local optometrists can test your child. This test is available in the UK under the NHS and is free for children under 16 (19 if they are in full time education).

By having regular check-ups (at least every two years), optometrists can pick up undetected visual problems. The majority of children will have perfectly healthy eyes but some may not be able to focus properly, leading to learning difficulties. These problems can be remedied by spectacles and therefore sorted out very quickly.

In recent years, glasses have often been used as a 'fashion statement', making it much easier for children to select glasses they like and to not feel the 'odd one out'.

However, if there is a more serious problem which the orthoptic feels needs further investigation, they can refer your child to the orthoptic department at your local hospital.

These specialists can use a variety of screening tests, including:

- Specialist eye tests.
- Intuitive Colorimeter (coloured overlays).
- Vision training (see chapter 16).
- Dunlop Test (see chapter 16).

Coloured overlays and tinted glasses

Coloured overlays seem to work by filtering out light that causes distortions to print. The problems appear to be worse with black print on white paper. Students often report problems with eyestrain, migraine, etc.

Your child may benefit from glasses or lenses if, when reading, they find:

- Letters merge together.

- Letters appear in the wrong order.

- Twirling letters.

- Words are fuzzy.

- Words jump about.

- Difficulties in reading and keeping their place.

- Excessive rubbing and blinking of their eyes.

- Words appear as a jumbled puzzle.

- Words appear faded.

What can I do if my child has a problem?

If you suspect your child may have this problem, you can use a quick and simple screening test using Cerium Overlays (coloured sheets). These overlays are clear coloured plastic sheets that are placed over written work. When the overlays are placed over text, many students say 'the words have stopped jumping about'.

You can get these sheets in different colours and if you find they help then you can organise a full test at the optometrists using the Intuitive Colorimeter.

The Cerium Overlays and Screening Kit can be purchased through Cerium Visual Technologies.

What is an Intuitive Colorimeter?

The Intuitive Colorimeter uses up to 7,000 different tints to measure exactly which colour helps individual students to read better. Glasses are then made for students to use with reading and writing. Research has shown that if a child uses coloured overlays, his reading speed increases and he has fewer headaches.

Headlines like 'Experts hail cure for child dyslexia' and 'A miracle cure' have appeared in most national newspapers over the last few years. And they have all been talking about the wonderful success being achieved by scores of dyslexic students. The remarkable achievements have occurred after being prescribed vision training or tinted glasses.

While the 'miracle cure' may have helped some children with this particular problem, I cannot emphasise enough that it does not sort out the majority of children's eye problems. That is not to say it isn't worth trying – it definitely is.

Where can I get this test?

There are still only a few optometrists who have the Intuitive Colorimeter in their premises. The test is not available on the NHS at the moment. For a full list of participating optometrists, visit www.dyslexiaa2z.com.

Where can I get help with general sight-loss?

The Royal National Institute for the Blind (RNIB) provides a practical service to help people get on with their lives. Their aim is to give blind and partially sighted children the best possible start in life. With the right help, these children can perform as well as any other youngsters. They also campaign for integrated schooling (where applicable) and encourage greater public awareness of these problems.

Chronically Sick and Disabled Persons Act

If you have a child who has a hearing or sight loss, they may have rights under the Chronically Sick and Disabled Persons Act (1970). What a mouthful! Simply put, it means that local authorities have a duty to provide services to people with disabilities.

Before you can receive help, your child will need to have his needs correctly assessed. Contact your local social services for further information. The relevant social worker or doctor can arrange an assessment. If your child is assessed as requiring a service, the authority has a duty to provide it (although they may charge for this service).

If the local authority refuses to provide a service, you have every right to complain. In the first instance you should complain to the council itself (they all have complaints procedures in place so ask for a copy of them). If you do not have any success, contact the Citizens Advice Bureau or local government Ombudsman for assistance.

Vitamins and health

We know that if children do not have a well balanced diet of vitamins and minerals, it will show up with ill health. The government still says that we get all our vitamins and minerals from our food so there is no need to take pills.

As we spend so much time rushing around, grabbing processed and frozen meals, it may be that our children are missing out on the vital vitamins they need not only to grow but also to develop their mental capacities.

For further information on vitamins and supplements see chapter 18.

Summing Up

If your child is suffering from a medical problem, it stands to reason that he may not be able to hear/see what is being said, especially if he sits at the back of the classroom. Ensure that all medical checks have been carried out and then you will have peace of mind.

Role of the Orthoptist in Assessing Children with Specific Learning Difficulties (16)

By Christine Robinson (Mrs) DBO, SRO.

Children with specific learning difficulties may sometimes need to be referred to the orthoptist for a Dunlop Test. The tests carried out by the orthoptist help to analyse whether there are any contributory visual problems associated with the learning difficulties. Orthoptists are well qualified to undertake the testing of your child when there are specific learning difficulties. They are specially trained therapists who, among other things, assess vision for close work and distance and binocular function (how well the two eyes work together).

Some orthoptists have a special interest in assessing children with specific learning difficulties. They do not promise a miraculous cure if treatment is undertaken, but it may improve the visual information processing which can cause great problems for these children. Most of the children will still need specialised teaching.

How do I arrange referral to an orthoptist?

NHS referrals require a letter of introduction from your GP or the school doctor. Some orthoptists are happy to see private patients and in this instance a referral letter from your GP is not always essential. It is advisable to check the availability of these tests in your area as not all orthoptic departments are able to undertake this work.

What will the testing involve?

The Dunlop Test is one small part of your child's orthoptic assessment. The orthoptist will usually take a full case history, including details of any past treatment for eye problems.

The tests will include:

- Tests to eliminate the presence of a squint that causes 'cross eyes'.

- Checking of eye movements and ability to scan and pursue a moving target.

- Assessing the ability of the two eyes to look in together at a near point – i.e. convergence.

- Assessing the ability of both eyes to focus clearly on print at a near point, i.e. accommodation.

- Tests on stereoscopic vision – i.e. 3D vision.

- Tests on the reserves of muscle ability present to maintain comfortable use of both eyes together.

- The Dunlop Test – to determine whether there is a reference eye well established.

- Assessment with a selection of intuitive coloured overlays, if considered appropriate. If the child thinks one of the overlays helps, a rate of reading test is undertaken both with and without the choice filter.

- Assessment with the Dyslexia Research Trust's yellow and blue filters can also be given if considered appropriate.

The Dunlop Test

This test originated in Australia in 1971 and was designed by Mrs P. Dunlop, an orthoptist. Much research has been conducted in this country by Dr J. Stein, a physiologist, and Mrs S. Fowler, an orthoptist (Royal Berkshire Hospital, Reading).

The test involves looking into a special machine at pictures that help us to decide which eye is in charge of sending a message (in the form of a picture) to the language centre in the brain so the picture can be deciphered (i.e. into a word).

It is a two-eyed test – both eyes are open – and we learn whether a reference or lead eye is established.

This should not be confused with a dominant eye, which is tested when you hold a tube or kaleidoscope to one eye – invariably the other eye is automatically closed.

Will treatment be needed?

Once the tests are completed, your orthoptist will be able to discuss the findings with you.

If the vision is reduced, your child will need to see an optician or ophthalmologist (specialist eye doctor) to check that the eyes are healthy, and to have glasses ordered if necessary.

If there is no reference eye and the child is over seven, special glasses with one lens frosted over may be prescribed for all reading, writing and number work. This is not a self-help treatment and progress will need to be monitored carefully by your orthoptist. If your child already has a fixed reference eye then it is unlikely that frosted glasses will be needed.

Sometimes children with dyslexia need eye exercises to improve the accurate use of both eyes together at a near point. Indeed, they often admit that the words and letters move about or go fuzzy – they may not have commented on this as they think everyone else sees things in the same way!

If the intuitive coloured overlays are helpful, the child can be referred to an optometrist with a 'colorimeter' – this is a machine to determine the exact colour to be dispensed in tinted glasses. The advantage of glasses is that they can be used for writing as well as reading.

If a Dyslexia Research Trust filter is chosen, tinted glasses can be offered on loan for either of these colours.

Aims of treatment

- To develop a reference eye.

- To have a good ability to look in to a near point with both eyes together, and maintain a clear picture (convergence and accommodation).

- To have good smooth eye movements in scan and pursuit.

- To have good muscle reserves (fusional ability).

How long will treatment last?

If treatment is recommended, it could be as little as one month for exercises or up to a maximum of one year if frosted glasses are prescribed.

If a reference eye does not become established after a maximum of one year, treatment will be stopped.

If treatment is suggested, it is certainly worth a try as there is nothing to lose and it may prove to be extremely beneficial.

Christine Robinson (Mrs) DBO, SRO.
Senior orthoptist, Great Western Hospital, Swindon.

Optometric evaluation

By Keith Holland, B.Sc, FBCO, DCLP

In order to be able to concentrate, absorb information and maintain interest in the written word, the visual system of a young person has been developed with certain capabilities. The eyes have to be capable of moving smoothly and easily along a line of print, jumping back and down to the beginning of the next line and repeating this action for extended periods of time.

Students also have to be able to adjust the focus of their eyes rapidly from distance to near and back again when copying from a blackboard.

Conscious or subconscious?

It is important that these activities can be performed without conscious thought or effort. If the brain has to 'use up' concentration and energy in order to simply move the eyes along a line of print, then there is less likelihood that the contents of the text will have any meaning, that they will be remembered or that the words which are coming next are anticipated. Reading has to become a subconscious action.

Learning to read

Learning to move the eyes in a way which enables us to read efficiently is like changing gear – it's a learned action. Some young people fail to develop this skill and as a result their reading and writing ability is often lower than expected.

Other skills such as ball-catching or graceful gymnastic body movements can also be affected, and children with poorly developed vision systems are frequently observed to be clumsy and ill coordinated.

Behaviour optometry

Some fully qualified and state registered optometrists now additionally practice what is called behaviour optometry. Behaviour optometrists operate on the basis that visual skills are learned and therefore trainable.

Vision is considered to be an inseparable part of the whole human system and should not be regarded as a separate and individual function. This means that our behaviour and our environment can influence the way in which our visual system works, and vice versa.

Behavioural optometrists use activities and training to improve the efficiency of the whole visual system.

Vision training

Vision training or vision therapy provides a means of learning to use the visual system in a more efficient manner. When the visual system works more efficiently, more information can be received, processed and understood. When there are problems with visual perception and understanding vision input, achieving full potential can be helped by using the techniques of vision training.

This involves developing good body bilaterality, hand-eye coordination, form perception, directionality and visualisation skills, as well as ensuring that the muscles which focus and direct the eyes are functioning efficiently. Should vision training be necessary, these terms will become more meaningful as the therapy programme progresses.

Who can benefit?

Students with good visual abilities read faster with less effort, understand more of what they read and retain it longer. Athletes who use their vision effectively see things more quickly, more accurately and show good overall performance. The improvement in the processing of visual information can benefit many areas of life, especially at school, in sports and at work.

Optometric vision training is individually programmed to the specific needs of each patient, with the basic universally needed skills being included in all programmes. Other activities are designed to meet specific needs.

What to look for

Children who may benefit from vision training can often be seen when reading to have difficulty in keeping their place and in following lines of print.

Typically, a child will read with a finger or a marker under the line being read, and as they read they will move the whole of the head rather than simply following the print with their eyes. In many cases, mathematical ability and intelligence may be normal or higher than normal for the age, yet reading presents a problem.

The concentration span of a young person with a poorly developed visual system will often be very short. Time spent reading will come to an abrupt halt and a sudden complete lack of interest.

Who can help?

Obviously if a child has learning difficulties, all avenues of possible help have to be explored. In order to establish if there may be a visual component to the learning difficulty, a full eye examination must be carried out by an optometrist.

If it is suspected that there may be a developmental visual problem (in other words, all the bits are there and are healthy but are not coordinating properly), then your optometrist may wish to deal with this himself. Alternatively, you may choose to be referred to a behavioural optometrist who has more experience in helping with learning problems.

Where to go

The British Association of Behavioural Optometrists maintain a register of all optometrists who have attended a further education course specifically designed to develop their knowledge and skills.

Summing Up

The Dunlop Test and vision training have often seemed to be surrounded in mystery, but quite simply means fully testing the eyes and training them to respond to appropriate treatment. This treatment may take a few months or several years. If successful, it can be a tremendous help to the child. These tests are usually carried out in optometrist departments in hospitals rather than at your local opticians.

Education is Compulsory – Not School (17)

The majority of children in the UK go to school. However, they do not have to. It is education that is compulsory, not actually attending a school.

The law says that it is a parent's duty to cause their child to receive efficient full-time education suitable to his age, ability and aptitude, and to any special educational needs he may have, either by regular attendance at school or otherwise (Sylvia Jeffs 1996).

There are many reasons why some children do not go to school. Some of these include the following:

- Parents simply do not want to 'let go' of their children.

- Parents believe they can educate their children better than the state.

- Children with special needs need more attention than is available at some schools.

- Some schools have failed their children.

- Some children refuse to go to school.

- Some children are being bullied.

- Sometimes special dietary needs cannot be met at school.

- The child has been expelled.

- Religious reasons.

- The child is chronically ill.

If a child is already registered at a school, he must be de-registered in accordance with the Pupil's Registration Regulations. The parents must write to the headteacher to explain that they are home-educating, i.e. have already started teaching.

This is an automatic procedure for children at mainstream schools: after the headteacher receives written notification from the parent, he will notify the LEA.

Contrary to popular belief you do not need:

- Permission to educate your child outside school.

- To justify your decision.

- To inform the LEA (there are sometimes exceptions).

- To hold teaching qualifications.

- To follow the National Curriculum.

- To follow a specific syllabus.

- To follow a timetable.

- To follow school hours.

- To have formal school-type lessons.

Many LEAs are quite supportive of children being educated at home (unlike years ago) and offer valuable help, advice and equipment.

Education Otherwise is a leading organisation in helping and explaining people's rights to education at home. They have campaigned for higher recognition for many years. They have a wide range of books and booklets which explain your rights and duties and discuss the practicalities of dealing with educational authorities

Summing Up

We normally think that education is carried out only in schools, but for a variety of reasons there are a percentage of children who are educated outside these establishments. At all times we must remember that it is the parent's choice and not the LEA's.

It is the education that is compulsory, not school.

Vitamins and Health (18)

Most people would accept the premise that eating a balanced diet is essential to our children's mental and physical development. Many scientific studies have shown that a nutritionally complete diet is necessary in the development of vision, learning ability and coordination. But are our children getting a well balanced diet or should they be taking supplements? Can taking supplements of fatty acids, zinc and iron cure dyslexia, dyspraxia and ADHD? Many parents who use these supplements say a resounding 'yes', and there now appears to be strong evidence to support this.

One study indicated that children who had a decent breakfast before exams performed much better than those who skipped breakfast or just had a bowl of cereal. Another study showed that if a student ate a Mars bar directly before an exam, they also performed better (this is the only time I encouraged my boys to eat Mars bars). The most likely reason for these results is that the breakfast/chocolate provides a short-lived surge in blood glucose levels so brain functioning improves within a short period of time.

Fatty acids

There have been a lot of studies over the last decade which have concluded that abnormal levels of fatty acids in the brain could be behind the practical and behavioural problems experienced by dyslexic children, as well as those with dyspraxia and ADHD. (There is further information on the link between fatty acids and ADHD in chapter 8.)

Many parents of dyslexic, dyspraxic and ADHD children now give their children these supplements – some parents have seen remarkable results.

Many of the parents attending the Swindon Dyslexia Centre say that within a very short period of time their child is calmer, can concentrate better and has started to catch up with his reading and writing. This does not appear to help everyone but is certainly worth trying.

Michael – nine years

Dyslexic and ADHD

Michael has dyslexia and ADHD. He had severe literacy problems and found it difficult to concentrate and sit still for long.

Michael attended the Swindon Dyslexia Centre twice a week to help him with his problems. While they were there one day, his mother read an article on Efalex. She said she was desperate and 'willing to try anything'. Within weeks of Michael taking the tablets, she noticed a difference in his behaviour at home. The school also commented on his improvement in concentration span and behaviour.

Michael is now making steady progress with reading, writing and spelling, and can sit still for much longer periods.

His mother said: 'It is truly remarkable, certainly worth the money.'

Two of the products containing fatty acids are:

Efalex (liquid or tablets)

This provides the important long chain fatty acids, DHA and AA, needed to help maintain eye and brain function and the development of vision.

Eye q

This contains the long chain polyunsaturated fatty acids, EPA and DHA . Also included is GLA from EPArich marine oil and pure evening primrose oil. Long chain polyunsaturated fatty acids play an important role in the development of the eye and brain, especially vision, coordination, memory and concentration.

These supplements are now available as liquid, tablets or 'chews' which make them more palatable for children. They can be purchased from chemists, health shops and most large supermarkets.

Iron supplements

In a study published in November 1996, an American group of scientists said teenage girls improved if they were given iron supplements. Previous research appears to show that anaemia affects the mental abilities of children. Animal research has also hinted that iron deficiency is enough to change brain iron levels, which in turn alter the way neurotransmitters behave in the brain.

Zinc supplements

Zinc is one of our body's most important trace minerals and there has been some research to show that people with dyslexia have been linked to a deficiency of this mineral.

Zinc plays an important part in the body's immune system. A shortage can affect the healing process because the body is unable to store it, therefore it is vital that we eat enough zinc in our daily diet to stay healthy. An indicator of a lack of zinc includes white marks on fingernails and dandruff.

Zinc can be found in many foods, including:

- Lean meat.
- Liver.
- Cheddar cheese.

- Chicken.

- Eggs.

- Wholemeal breads.

- Whole grain cereals.

- Dried beans.

- Seafood.

Zinc can be destroyed or blocked by various things, including tannin (found in tea, coffee and alcohol), food colourings and additives.

Should we take supplements?

Most people agree that if our children eat a well balanced diet there is no need to take supplements and they will be healthy and well. However, that is not always possible when we are rushing around, trying to be all things to everyone.

Supplements can be a safe and effective way of ensuring children are getting the nutrients needed to help them keep healthy and aid their mood and concentration generally.

Summing Up

While the debate regarding vitamin supplements continues, the experts seem to disagree with each other constantly. Some argue that if our children receive a well balanced diet, they do not need to take vitamin supplements. Others say that with vitamin supplements, children who are deficient in some areas of their diet will make faster progress.

Without any concrete evidence and guidance from the government, the decision has to be left to you.

Career Options (19)

Further education/career choices

Thinking about career choices while still at school is extremely daunting for the student and the decision made at this stage may affect their whole working life. However, our experiences at school, college and in the workplace make us consider our career choices regularly throughout our working lives. These days it is unusual to have a job for life and we have to continue to change over the years.

Careers advice

The Careers Office covers all areas of the country, although their name has recently been changed (the name is different all over the country). However, they are still available nationwide to advise you or your child on their future educational needs. The Careers Office holds vast, up-to-date information on hundreds of jobs.

During the last two years at school, careers advisers go into schools to talk to students. Every student will have the opportunity of an in-depth interview with a careers adviser. The interview will be centred on your child and will discuss his strengths, interests and ambitions. It will also explain the education and training options open to him. Once this has been completed, a Careers Guidance Plan can then be developed which will summarise the meeting and the steps agreed.

The student will then have to make a decision about which way he would like to go:

- Further academic studies, e.g. A Level or further GCSEs.

- Vocational course – work related courses/GNVQs.

- Specific training or employment.

Assessment support at employment centres

All job centres have a registered person who is referred to as a disability employment adviser (DEA). This person is the 'gatekeeper' to specialist vocational support for people with disabilities. They will have a great deal of experience and, more importantly, understanding of people with learning difficulties in the work situation.

Dyslexia is a registered disability under the Chronically Sick and Disabled Persons Act 1970, Education Act 1993 and the Disability Discrimination Act 1995. All employment centres have been provided with a comprehensive description of dyslexia.

New Deal programme

People who are dyslexic and unemployed are allowed to go into the New Deal programme early. If they have problems, the disability employment adviser will establish what is causing a barrier to employment. If necessary, the DEA can refer the young person to a psychologist for further testing. They may also be able to offer further numeracy and literacy training as part of the gateway provision within the New Deal programme.

The Adult Literacy Service

The Adult Literacy Service works with your LEA and provides advice and information to students with learning disabilities. The Further Education Funding Council may be able to give additional funding to students with special educational needs. Colleges try to ensure that there are equal opportunities for all potential students.

Psychometric testing

Psychometric testing can help all students and is sometimes arranged in school in conjunction with the careers adviser. The testing includes comprehensive assessments that can be carried out in writing or on a computer. The tests provide an objective assessment of an individual's abilities and personality, matching them to possible career choices held on a computer. It analyses the student's personal information and interests, then suggests career choices they may not have thought of. There are many different types of tests around but they are all similar.

Is it worth having a psychometric test?

We spend between 25% and 33% of our time at work so it is very important to find a job you like. If your child chooses a career that does not suit them, they will soon become unhappy. No one wants a job they hate. So why not take the time to find a job that suits your personality?

Psychometric testing can help you find a job:

- You are suited to.

- Which gives you job satisfaction.

- That encourages you to contribute something to the success of the company.

These tests are also available in some libraries, colleges and educational establishments, in some private companies and online. Some of these are free for a short test and others charge for an in-depth test. Either way, they are worthwhile and sometimes come up with some interesting facts.

Two companies providing these tests are www.psychometrics.com/onlinetests and www.psychometricadvantage.co.uk.

Summing Up

A lot of help and advice is now given to students at school. This starts when the pupils are approximately 13/14 years of age and continues until they leave school. This ensures that the pupil has been given the option of different career choices available to them.

Psychometric testing is now widely available at some schools, colleges, universities and career offices, and this can be used as a great tool for the person with special needs.

Dyslexia and the Disability Discrimination Act (DDA) (20)

Dyslexia and the Disability Discrimination Act

Dyslexia is a registered disability under the Chronically Sick and Disabled Persons Act 1970, Education Act 1993 and the Disability Discrimination Act (DDA) 1995.

In order to get the best from your staff it is important that you understand exactly what dyslexia is. By understanding the condition you will be able to support your dyslexic employees.

What does the law say?

Under this Act, the law requires you to make 'reasonable adjustments' for certain employees with difficulties at work. These can often be just minor changes to the working place to make it easier for individual members of your staff.

How many of your staff and customers are dyslexic?

How many of your staff are dyslexic? Do you know what dyslexia is and how you can make reasonable adjustments to help those who are dyslexic? By understanding what dyslexia is you will be able to support your dyslexic employees. Sometimes just minor adjustments in the workplace can make it easier for your staff. Dyslexia affects 10% of the population. Therefore this is likely to have an impact, not just on your staff, but also on 10% of your customers, suppliers and delivery people, indeed everyone you come into contact with!

What is dyslexia?

Dyslexia affects 10% of the population, 4% severely. Problems can show themselves in reading, writing, number work, short-term memory, hand control and visual processing. Timekeeping, sense of direction and interpersonal skills can also be affected.

Many people with dyslexia are extremely bright in lots of ways, always talking and asking questions, but they do not seem to reach their full potential in the academic field. (For a full description on dyslexia, please see chapter 3.)

*Dyslexia, Employers and the Disability Discrimination Act

The key points relating to dyslexia and employment are:

■ The Disability Discrimination Act 1995 (Amendment) Regulations 2003 came into force on 1 October 2004.

■ Since 2004, all businesses, with the exception of the Armed Forces, must comply with the Disability Discrimination Act.

■ Under the Disability Act (DDA) it is unlawful to treat a disabled applicant or employee less favourably because of their disability without justification.

■ Severe dyslexia is used as an example in several sections of the Code of Practice and fits the definition of disability used within the DDA.

*British Dyslexia Association, Dyslexia Contact January 2004.

What is a user-friendly workplace?

Trying to create a 'user-friendly' workplace is good practice. Many dyslexics do not need a lot of adjustments to their working environment but often small changes can really help. Many of these changes are simple and inexpensive.

As an employer you can help by:

- letting prospective employees apply online for job applications.

- making application forms easy (why not get a dyslexic employee to help design/change one or ask for help from a dyslexia charity?).

- using computer typeface in a font like Arial 12 to help make things easier to read.

- using pastel coloured paper wherever possible.

- highlighting important information in documents.

On computers:

- consider whether a laptop would be more suitable for the employee.

- make sure you can change the background colour on the screen.

- encourage the employee to make the font size larger if it will help.

- use speech to text software.

- ensure there are spelling and grammar checkers installed.

- use reminders on computers for important meetings, etc.

Other gadgets include:

- electronic organisers.

- palmtop computers.

- dictaphones.

- tape recorders.

- talking calculators – excellent for people with number problems.

Generally in the workplace:

- use voice mail rather than memos.

- keep the room quiet and away from distractions.

- use large boards above desks to remind employees of important dates.

If additional costs are required, such as a voice-activated computer, the employer can apply for funding through the Government's Access to Work (AtW) scheme.

Access to Work Scheme (AtW)

The Access to Work Scheme (AtW) is operated through your local JobCentre Plus office. Access to Work can help you if your health or disability affects the way you do your job. It gives you and your employer advice and support with extra costs which may arise because of your needs.

You may need to have an occupational health assessment carried out. This can be arranged via the local health authority (LHA) or under the Access to Work scheme. The assessment will then identify and recommend areas to enable the dyslexic employee to benefit in the workplace.

Once a need is identified, the Right to Work scheme can pay for part of the adjustments. Employers (company bosses) are required to share part of the cost with the AtW by paying the first £300 plus a further minimum 20% of the cost up to £10,000. They may be able to offset this cost against tax.

Access to Work will pay 100% of the approved costs if you are:

- self-employed.

- unemployed and starting a new job.

- working for an employer and have been in a job for less than six weeks.

- have people changing jobs in your company.

Whatever the employment status, Access to Work will also pay 100% of the approved costs of help with:

- support workers.

- fares to work.

- communicator support at interview.

In all these cases the employer orders the products, listed by the Access to Work scheme, and pays for them. They then claim the amount back off Access to Work. This scheme may be able to pay for equipment, adapting premises or for a support worker.

Occupational health assessments

An occupational health assessment can be carried out by your local health authority or under the Access to Work scheme.

There are several types of tests available:

- Occupational health assessment.

- Dyslexia screening assessment.

- Educational psychologist's report.

These assessments are very useful because it may be that the employee has never been identified as dyslexic, and the report would be able to identify specific work areas that would help him.

Where can I get further information?

The organisations below can send you further information.

- For information on the Right to Work (RtW) scheme contact your local JobCentre Plus office.

- For a leaflet on the Disability Discrimination Act, go online and visit www.direct.gov.uk or write to Disability on the Agenda.

- The British Dyslexia Association (BDA) has an information pack available, An Employer's Guide to Dyslexia, for £20.

- The Adult Dyslexia Organisation (ADO) also has a website with comprehensive information for employers.

See the help list at the back of the book for contact details.

Summing Up

As this is quite new legislation, it is obvious that not everyone will know what to do about all of the things mentioned above. However, the British Dyslexia Association (BDA) and the Adult Dyslexia Organisation (ADO) have very useful information packs available to employers free of charge. There is no excuse for employers who do not to take up this offer, especially when they can get most of the 'reasonable adjustments' paid for.

Legal Advice (21)

Sometimes, when parents have tried everything to get the help they need for their child, things still do not work out. It is on these occasions when they feel there is absolutely nothing further to do that they may decide to seek legal help.

The Education Acts 1993 and 1996 were set up to help children with special educational needs. These acts set up the Special Educational Needs Tribunal system, to which parents can appeal if they are not satisfied with the provision provided by their LEA. This is an independent organisation aimed at helping parents.

One former pupil, Pamela Phelps, 26, successfully sued the London Borough of Hillingdon and was awarded over £46,000 because they failed to diagnose her dyslexia.

There are now specialist firms offering legal advice to people who have had difficulties, for whatever reason, with their LEAs, colleges, etc. When looking for a company, please ensure the legal firms are registered with the Education Law Association. The Law Society regulates these associations.

These companies can usually provide legal representation on all aspects of education law, including:

■ Information about assessments and statementing.

■ Statementing procedures.

■ Enforcement of statements.

■ Special educational needs.

■ Special Educational Needs Tribunals.

■ Admission to schools you have chosen.

■ Dealing with a school that wants to reduce the teaching time/ therapy for your child.

■ Finding suitable experts for diagnosis of your child's needs.

- Advice regarding provision from the LEA or school.

- Independent school placements.

- Exclusion.

- School refusals.

- Dealing with bullying.

- Home tuition.

- Help for students whose schools have failed them.

Help Section (22)

Setting up a support group

I receive hundreds of calls each year asking how you go about setting up a support group.

It is not difficult at all. We all need help and support at some time or another. When your child has special needs, it is easy to feel as if you are the only one in the world with difficulties. There are thousands of children who have problems with their education. Parents need to come together to talk their problems through – to help and advise each other. Your problem will not be a new one. If you are suffering because of it, you can bet there are others out there in the same position.

Why not set up a support group?

Why not form a support group in your area? It isn't as hard as you may think! If you need support, there must be others feeling the same. Don't wait until someone else does it – because they might not!

How do I go about it?

- Ask other parents to see if they are interested in joining.

- Visit your local library, Citizens' Advice Bureau or other voluntary agencies to see if they have any information that may help you.

- Ask yourself, what exactly is needed in your area?

- Do you want to have meetings every week/month?

- Where will your meetings be? (It might be best to hold the first meeting in a local hall.)

- Contact the national charity to see what help they can offer.

■ Try to get a guest speaker for your first meeting from a national organisation.

Ask other parents to give you a hand. If you don't ask, you don't get; that is my maxim – you can't do everything yourself! It may seem hard at the start but keep going – it gets easier.

Advertising your group?

No, I don't mean by paying for advertisements with the local press. My company does not have an advertising budget at all. The local radio and newspapers need local news – let them know what you are doing. Just contact them by email, letter or telephone. Don't forget local news is their business!

Press release

The quickest way to let the press know is by a press release. Don't panic. This is very easy. It is just like writing a letter and then taking out all the chitchat, leaving just the bones. Something similar to the example opposite will be sufficient.

Maria Chivers

1 Any Road

Any Town

Any County

0123 454678

Press Release

Dyslexia Support Group

There will be a meeting in West Drayton School Hall, on Wednesday 17th November at 7.30, to discuss the setting up of a Support Group for Dyslexia.

There will be a guest speaker, from the British Dyslexia Association who will talk on 'Special Educational Needs – How you can help'.

The aim is to form a group for parents and carers, providing support and information about services in our area. There will be a small entrance fee of £1.00. Refreshments will be available.

For further information, please contact Maria Chivers,

Tel. 0123 45678.

****

Don't forget: if you need help, so do other people in the same situation!

Summing Up

I do not usually advocate people taking legal action, but we have to acknowledge the occasions when LEAs have let some children down and it has become necessary for parents to take things further.

I would just like to emphasise that parents who have problems do try to sort things out with the respective schools and LEAs before they get to this position. At the end of the day, any monies awarded to children have to come out of the education budget – leaving less money in the pot – so it really is a doublw edged sword.

And finally . . .

If we learn one thing from our research into dyslexia it is that early identification has got to be the key. Once you identify a child as having a learning difficulty and rule out any medical problems, you can start working towards a solution – before that child starts to fail!

I hope I have answered many of your questions about dyslexia and other learning difficulties. Unfortunately, there is no magic cure or secret formula, but there is a lot of help and advice available. I hope I have shown how you could use this to help your child. Check out my site on www.dyslexiaa2z.com for more information.

The British Dyslexia Association is 35 years old but there is still a need for more public and professional recognition of the problem. Voluntary groups, awareness weeks, conferences and the like all help to achieve this, and we can all support these. By joining the British Dyslexia Association you will receive up-to-date newsletters and information about the latest ideas in the dyslexia world. It is well worth a few pounds a year for membership – the stronger they are, the more they can get things changed in schools, colleges and the workplace.

I wish you all the best and good luck to you all.

Dyslexia A2Z.com

For all your dyslexia requirements, look at my website www.dyslexiaa2z.com.

Dyslexia A2Z has information on the following:

- Dyslexia assessments and tests.
- Dyscalculia (maths) assessments and tests.
- Dysgraphia (hand-writing) assessments and tests.
- Dyslexia tutors.
- Psychologists.
- Dyslexia tutors.
- Alternative therapists.
- Complementary therapists.
- Irlen syndrome.
- Intuitive Colorimeter.
- Efalex.
- Books on dyslexia, dyscalculia, dysgraphia, etc.
- Specialist software.
- ChromaGen.
- Phono-Graphix.
- NLP.
- NDD.
- ARROW.
- And more . . .

Don't Let Dyslexia Get You Down

More than 100 pupils from Seaford College in West Sussex, aged 10 – 18, have recorded a CD. The idea was to dispel some of the myths surrounding dyslexia, and the lyrics pay tribute to celebrities who have succeeded despite their learning difficulties.

The song has been written by the school's head of learning support, Nick Foster, with music composed and arranged by the school's head of RE, Richard Bailey.

Proceeds from the sale of the CDs will go towards two charities.

Don't let dyslexia get you down,

Look at the famous ones who have found

Their own dyslexia is no big deal,

And that is now how you can really feel.

Dyslexia's no big deal.

Don't let dyslexia get to you,

Look at the many things you can do.

The world won't stop if your spelling's not great.

Just use a spell checker, or even dictate.

Have confidence and create.

Look at the great Albert Einstein,

What a genius, what a mind.

Charles Darwin – the first man to state that

Humans are descended from the ape.

Look at the great Winston Churchill

Who led this country with such skill.

Thomas Edison got it right,

Invented the bulb and gave us light.

Now who could be much sexier

Than Tom Cruise with dyslexia?

Whoopi Goldberg and the singer Cher,

Successful entertainers and millionnaires.

Now Leonardo da Vinci

Earned his place in history,

A brilliant artist, an inventor too,

An exceptional man is the popular view.

He achieved success and you can do that too.

Help List

A2Z

www.dyslexiaa2z.com
This website was set up to help people find information on dyslexia in one place. Details on a wide range of things are included: teachers, psychologists, therapists, vitamins and supplements.

ACE (Advisory Centre for Education Ltd)

1c Aberdeen Studios, 22 Highbury Grove, London, N5 2DQ
Tel: 0808 800 5793
www.ace-ed.org.uk
Advice on education to parents and schools – produces a wide range of publications.

ADO (Adult Dyslexia Organisation)

336 Brixton Road, London, SW9 7AAA
Tel: 0207 924 9559
www.futurenet.co.uk/charity/ado/adomenu.htm
The ADO offers information, support, counselling and advice. They also have a comprehensive guide on employment and dyslexia.

ARROW Tuition Ltd

Arrow Centre, Bridgewater College, Cannington Court, Cannington, Somerset, TA5 2HA
Tel: 01278 652863
www.self-voice.com

Arts Dyslexia Trust (ADT)

14 Church Field Way, Wye, Ashford, Kent, TN25 5EQ
Tel: 01233 811960
www.artsdyslexiatrust.org.

AVP

School Hill Centre, Chepstow, Gwent, NP16 5PH
Tel: 01291 625 439

www.avp.co.uk
Specialist computer programs.

Back in Action

www.backinaction.co.uk
A portable seat wedge that converts to a writing slope. See website for office telephone numbers.

Basic Skills Agency (now moved to NIACE)

National Institute of Adult Continuing Education, 20 Princess Road West, Leicester, LE1 6TP
Tel: 0116 204 4200
www.niace.org.uk

BABO (British Association of Behavioural Optometrists)

Tel: 029 2022 8144
www.babo.co.uk
Register of members who are verified as having met the requirements for continuing education in behaviour optometry.

British Deaf Association

www.bda.org.uk
Contains the latest information about the deaf association and sign language. See website for UK offices.

British Dyslexia Association

Unit 8, Bracknell Beeches, Old Bracknell Lane, Bracknell, RG12 7BW
Tel: 0845 251 9002
www.bdadyslexia.org.uk
Aims to advance education and employment opportunities for people with dyslexia. Advice available on identification, teaching, etc. Wide list of books, brochures and software available.

Bristol Dyslexia Centre

10 Upper Belgrave Road, Clifton, Bristol, BS8 2XH

Tel: 0117 973 9405
www.dyslexiacentre.co.uk
Specialist software 'Nessy' has been developed by the centre.

Calibre

New Road, Weston Turville, Aylesbury, Buckinghamshire, HP22 5XQ
Tel: 01296 432 339
www.calibre.org.uk
Books for coursework and examinations on tape.

Children's Legal Centre

University of Essex, Wivenhoe Park, Colchester, CO4 3SQ
Tel: 01206 872 466
www.childrenslegalcentre.com
A unique, independent national charity concerned with law and policy affecting children and young people.

Citizens Advice Bureau (CAB)

115-123 Pentonville Road, London, N1 9LZ
Tel: 020 7833 2181 (admin only – no advice)
www.nacab.org.uk

Community Legal Advice

www.communitylegaladvice.org.uk
Website set up to provide people with free, confidential legal advice.

CReSTeD (Council for the Registration of Schools Teaching Dyslexic Pupils)

Greygarth, Littleworth, Winchcombe, Cheltenham, Gloucestershire, GL54 5BT
Tel: 01242 604 852
www.crested.org.uk
CReSTeD maintain a Register of Schools for dyslexic children.

Department for Children, Schools and Families

(formally Department for Education and Skills)
Sanctuary Buildings, Great Smith Street, London, SW1P 3BT
Tel: 0870 000 2288
www.dcsf.gov.uk
Government department set up to assist parents and professionals
with all aspects of education and employment.

The Disability Discrimination Act

Disability on the Agenda, Freepost, Bristol, BS38 7DE
www.disability.gov.uk

Disability Equality in Education

Unit IM, Leroy House, 436 Essex Road, London, N1 3QP
Tel: 020 7359 2855
www.diseed.org.uk

Dyscovery Centre

Alltyryn Campus, University of Wales, Newport, NP20 5DA
Tel: 01633 432330
www.dyscovery.co.uk
Provides a specialist and high quality service helping individuals
with living and learning difficulties.

Dyslexia Action

Head Office, Park House, Wick Road, Egham, Surrey, TW20 0HH
Tel: 01784 222 300
www.dyslexiaaction.org.uk
Main functions are assessment and tuition in their 26 centres,
and teacher training. They also carry out research and develop
specialist teaching materials.

Dyslexia Association of Ireland

Suffolk Chambers, 1 Suffolk Street, Dublin 2, Ireland
Tel: 01679 0276
www.dyslexia.ie
Aims to promote awareness of SpLDs/dyslexia.

Dyslexia Research Trust

See website for clinic contact details.
www.dyslexic.org.uk
Plenty of information, mainly on vision problems and fatty acids.

Dyspraxia Foundation

8 West Alley, Hitchin, Hertfordshire, SG5 1EG
Tel: 01462 454 986
www.dyspraxiafoundation.org.uk
This registered charity offers help and advice on dyspraxia. Lots of publications available.

The Educational Grants Directory

Directory of Social Change, 24 Stephenson Way, London, NW 2DP
Tel: 020 7391 4800
www.dsc.org.uk
Independent source of information and support to voluntary and community sectors.

Education Otherwise

PO Box 325, King's Lynn, PE34 3XW
www.educationotherwise.org
Provides support and information for families whose children are being educated outside school.

Educational Psychologists (Association of)

26, The Avenue, Durham, DH1 4ED
Tel: 01913 849 512
www.aep.org.uk
This association represents the majority of qualified educational psychologists who work in England, Wales and Northern Ireland.

Gamz

25 Albert Park Road, Malvery, Worcestershire, WR14 1HW
Tel: 01684 562 158
www.gamzuk.com
Literacy games for dyslexics and others.

Gifted Children's Information Centre

Dr Peter J Congdon PhD, MA (Ed), BA
Hampton Grange, 21 Hampton Lane, Solihull, B91 2QJ
Tel: 021 705 4547
www.ukselfhelp.info/giftedchildren
Help and advice available to parents and professionals in identifying 'gifted' children. Publishes a series of leaflets and handbooks.

Harcourt Assessment (now Pearson Assessment)

Halley Court, Jordan Hill, Oxford, OX2 8EJ
Tel: 01865 888 188
www.pearson-uk.com
Handwriting Without Tears and specialist testing equipment.

Helen Arkell Dyslexia Centre

Frensham, Farnham, Surrey, GU10 3BW
Tel: 01252 792 400
www.arkellcentre.org.uk
A registered charity offering expert assessment and specialist tuition to anyone with dyslexia or other SpLDs.

Hyperactive Children's Support Group (HACSG)

Dept W, 71 Whyke Lane, Chichester, West Sussex, PO19 7PD
www.hacsg.org.uk

IANSYST Ltd

Fen House, Fen Road, Chesterton, Cambridge, CB4 1UN
Tel: 01223 420 101
www.iansyst.co.uk
Catalogue available for thousands of specialist equipment, including computer software, etc.

Independent Schools Council Information Services (ISCIS)

Independent Schools Council, St Vincent House, 30 Orange Street, London, WC2H 7HH
Tel: 020 7766 7070

www.isis.org.uk
Associations of independent schools in the UK.

Insight Medical Products

Units 1-4 Silk Mill Studios, 2 Charlton Road, Tetbury,
Gloucestershire, GL8 8DY
Tel: 01666 500055
www.insightmedical.net

IPSEA (Independent Panel for Special Education Advice)

6 Carlow Mews, Woodbridge, Suffolk, IP12 1EA
Tel: 0800 018 4016
www.ipsea.org.uk
Gives independent, expert advice about special education.

Keith Holland Optometrist

27 St George's Road, Cheltenham, GL50 3DT
Tel: 01242 233 500
www.keithholland.co.uk
Specialist eye-care team in the treatment of children with learning disabilities.

Keytools (BigKeys)

Abacus House, 1 Spring Crescent, Southampton, SO17 2FZ
Tel: 023 8029 4500
www.keytools.co.uk
Range of inclusive computer access equipment for special needs.

LDA Living & Learning

Tel: 0845 120 4776
www.ldalearning.com
Wide selection of specialist software and products. Catalogue available.

Listening Books

12 Lant Street, London, SE1 1QH

Tel: 020 7407 9417
www.listening-books.org.uk
Books for coursework and examinations on tape.

The Left-Handed Shop

18 Avenue Road, Belmont, Surrey, SM2 6JD
Tel: 020 8770 3722
www.anythingleft-handed.co.uk
Information and products for left-handers.

Local Government Ombudsman

See website for addresses.
Tel: 0845 602 1983
www.lgo.org.uk
Government Ombudsman set up to look into complaints from people about various matters including Education Appeal Committees.

LUCID

3 Spencer Street, Beverley, East Yorkshire, HU17 9EG
Tel: 01482 882 121
www.lucid-research.com
Computerised testing equipment for dyslexia.

Mensa Limited (British)

St John's House, St John's Square, Wolverhampton, WV2 4AH
Tel: 01902 772 771
www.mensa.org.uk

Mental Health Foundation

London Office: 9th Floor, Sea Containers House, 20 Upper Ground, London, SE1 9QB.
Tel: 020 780 3 1101
Scotland Office: Merchants House, 30 George Square, Glasgow, G2 1EG.
Tel: 0141 572 0125
www.mhf.org.uk

Information service, leaflets and publications available.

The National Academy for Gifted and Talented Youth

The University of Warwick, Coventry, CV4 7AL
Tel: 024 7657 4427
The academy works with parents, teachers and LEAs to shape the provision of additional support for gifted and talented pupils.

National Association for the Gifted Child

NAGC, Suite 14, Challenge House, Sherwood Drive, Bletchley, Bucks, MK3 6DP
Tel: 0845 450 0295
www.nagcbritain.org.uk
NAGC has newsletters and publications for the gifted child.

National Association for Special Educational Needs (NASEN)

Nasen House, 4/5 Amber Business Village, Amber Close, Amington, Tamworth,
Staffs, B77 4RP
Tel: 01827 311 500
www.nasen.org.uk

National Blind Children's Society

Bradbury House, Market Street, Highbridge, Somerset, TA9 3BW (admin)
2nd Floor, Shawton House, 792 Hagley Road, Quinton, Birmingham, B68 0PJ (advice)
Tel: 01278 764 764 (admin) 01278 764771 (advice)
www.nbcs.org.uk

National Deaf Children's Society

15 Dufferin Street, London, EC1Y 8UR
Tel: 0808 800 8880
www.ndcs.org.uk
Helps families, parents and carers to maximise their skills and abilities.

National Federation of Access Centres (now National Network of Assessment Centres)

www.nnac.org

UK network of specialist services that work together to facilitate access for disabled people to education, training and personal development.

National Federation of the Blind of the UK

Sir John Wilson House, 215 Kirkgate, Wakefield, West Yorkshire, WF1 1JG

Tel: 01924 291313

www.nfbuk.org

Organisation to make life easier for blind/partially blind people.

National Handwriting Association

www.nha-handwriting.org.uk

Network 81

1-7 Woodfield Terrace, Chapel Hill, Stansted, Essex, CM24 8AJ

Tel: 0870 770 4055

www.network81.org

This national network of parents advises parents about special needs provision and statementing.

NFER-NELSON (now GL Assessment)

The Chiswick Centre, 414 Chiswick High Road, London, W4 5TF

Tel: 020 8996 8445

www.gl-assessment.co.uk

Provides specialist resources and testing equipment for special needs.

Pearson Assessment

Halley Court, Jordan Hill, Oxford, OX2 8EJ (customer services)

Tel: 0845 6308888 (8.00am - 5.00pm, Monday to Friday)

info@psychcorp.co.uk

www.psychcorp.co.uk

Penfriend XP LTD

30 South Oswald Road, Edinburgh, EH9 2HG
Tel: 0131 668 2000
www.penfriend.biz

Portage Service (National Portage Association)

Kings Courrt, 17 School Road, Hall Green, Birmingham, B28 8JG
www.portage.org.uk

Pre-School Learning Alliance (formerly Playgroup Association)

The Fitzpatrick Building, 188 York Way, London, N7 9AD
Tel: 020 7697 2500
www.pre-school.org.uk
This national educational charity advises about pre-school and education.

Psychological Corporation (now part of Pearson Assessment)

Halley Court, Jordan Hill, Oxford, OX2 8EJ
Tel: 0845 630 8888
www.psychcorp.co.uk
Catalogue for specialist testing for educational psychologists, schools, etc.

Pullen Publications (now Able Children Ltd)

13 Station Road, Knebworth, Herts, SG3 6AP.
Tel: 01438 814316.
www.literacytrust.org.uk/database/able.html
Specialises in books for able pupils.

REM

Great Western House, Langport, Somerset, TA10 9YU
Tel: 01458 254 700
www.r-e-m.co.uk/rem
Leading independent supplier of educational software.

Royal College of Speech and Language Therapists

2 White Hart Yard, London, SE1 1NX
Tel: 020 7378 1200
www.rcslt.org

RNIB (Royal National Institute for the Blind)

105 Judd Street, London, WC1H 9NE
Tel: 0845 766 9999/ 020 7388 2525
Typetalk: 0800 515152
www.rnib.org.uk
Leading charity working for blind and partially sighted people.

RNID (Royal National Institute for Deaf People)

19-23 Featherstone Street, London, EC1Y 8SL
Tel: 0800 808 0123
Textphone: 0800 808 9000
www.rnid.org.uk
This leading charity campaigns for improvements in facilities and services.

SEMERC

Angel House, Sherston, Malmesbury, Wiltshire, SN16 0LH
Tel: 01666 843200 (sales)
01666 843293 (technical enquiries)
www.semerc.com

SEN Legal

9 Looms Lane, Bury St Edmunds, Suffolk, IP33 1HE
Tel: 01284 723952
www.senlegal.co.uk
Legal firm specialising in education law and special needs.

SEN Marketing

618 Leeds Road, Outerwood, Wakefield, WF1 2LT
Tel: 01924 871697
www.senbooks.co.uk
Specialist software catalogue available.

SKILL

4th Floor, Chapter House, 18-20 Crucifix Lane, London, SE1 3JW
Tel: 020 7450 0620
Info Line: 0800 328 5050
www.skill.org.uk
National Bureau for students with disabilities in post-16 education, promoting opportunities in training and employment across the UK.

Society for Italic Handwriting (SIH)

Nick Caulkin, 203 Dyas Avenue, Great Barr, Birmingham B42 1HN
Tel: 0121 244 8006 (evenings/weekends only)
www.nickthenibs.co.uk/calligraphy.htm
nickthenibs@hotmail.co.uk

Special Educational Needs and Disability Tribunal

SENDIST, Procession House, 55 Ludgate Hill, London, EC4M 7JW
Tel: 0870 241 2555 (helpline)
Tel: 0870 606 5750 (discrimination helpline)
www.sendist.gov.uk

Book List

ADHD

ADHD, Research Practice and Opinion
Edited by Paul Cooper and Katherine Bilton, University of Cambridge.

Hyperactive Child
By Belinda Barnes, Foresight, £5.95.

Dyslexia

Adult Dyslexia: Assessment, Counselling and Training
By David McLoughlin, Gary Fitzgibbon and Vivienne Young, WHURR.

Brian Has Dyslexia – A Dr Spot Case Book
By Jenny Leigh, Red Kite Books.
Helps explain to very young children what dyslexia is.

Catch 'em Young
By Judith Stansfield.

Dealing with Dyslexia
By Pat Heaton and Patrick Winterson, WHURR.

Dyslexia a Hundred Years On
By TR Miles and Elaine Miles, Open University Press.

Dyslexia: An Introductory Guide
By James Doyle, WHURR.

Dyslexia and Alternative Therapies
By Maria Chivers, JKP Essentials

Dyslexia, Dyspraxia and Mathematics
By Dorian Yeo, Emerson House, London.

Dyslexia, Speech and Language: A Practitioner's Handbook
Edited by Margaret Snowling and Joy Stackhouse, WHURR.

Dyslexia, The Inner Hurt
Edited by Maria Chivers, Forward Press, 1995.

Every Letter Counts
By Susan Hampshire, Bantam Books,1990.

Growing Up With Dyslexia
By Margaret Newton, NAMCW.

How to Detect and Manage Dyslexia
By Philomena Ott.

How Dyslexics Learn Grasping the Nettle
By Dr Kate Saunders and Annie White, PATOSS.

Introduction to Dyslexia
By Lindsay Peer and Gavin Reid.

Overcoming Dyslexia
By Dr. Beve Hornsby, Macdonald & Co, London.

Practical Strategies for Living with Dyslexia
By Maria Chivers, Jessica Kingsley.

Susan's Story
By Susan Hampshire, Bantam Press.

Tackling Dyslexia
By Ann Cooke, WHURR, 2002.

The Gift of Dyslexia
By Ronald Davis and Eldon Braun.

This Book Doesn't Make Sense
By Jean Augur, Better Books & Software Ltd.

Understanding Dyslexia
By TR Miles.

Dyspraxia

Developmental Dyspraxia
By Madeleine Portwood, David Fulton. A practical manual for parents and professionals.

Dyspraxia: The Hidden Handicap
By Dr Amanda Kirby, Souvenir Press.

Living with Dyspraxia – A Guide for Adults
By Mary Colley.

Praxis Makes Perfect 11
A Dyspraxia Foundation publication, an essential guide for parents and teachers.

Dyscalculia

Butterworth B
Dyscalculia screener, Nfer-nelson, 2003.

Mathematics for Dyslexics – A Teaching Handbook
By S Chin & R Ashcroft, WHURR.

Mathematics Solutions – An Introduction to Dyscalculia
By Jan Poustie et al, Next Generation. Teaching tips and resources.

Steps Ahead in Dyscalculia
By Cowell & Chivers, 2009. This is the workbook to go with the Steps Ahead in Dyscalculia Scheme also by Cowell & Chivers. The Scheme also has a dyscalculia test; details can be found online at www.dyslexiaa2z.com.

Dysgraphia

Dysgraphia and Other Learning Difficulties – A Parent's Guide
By Maria Chivers, DyslexiaA2Z.com.

Handwriting Rescue Kit
By Pippa Chudley, REM.

Handwriting Without Tears
By Molly Shannon, OTR/L., Harcourt Assessment.

Why Johnny Can't Write
By Diane Walton, Cavey Pub, Pro Ed. A handbook for teachers and parents.

Education Otherwise

Home Education & The Law
By David Deutsch and Kolya Wolf, 19 New Cross Road, Oxford, OX3 8LP.

Giftedness

Assessing Gifted and Talented Children
Carolyn Richardson, The Qualifications and Curriculum Authority.

Working with gifted and talented children: Key Stages 1 and 2 English and mathematics
Contact QCA publications on 01787 884444.

Need - 2 - Know

Other Large Print Titles Include ...

Allergies A Parent's Guide
ISBN 978-1-86144-160-7 £12.99

Autism A Parent's Guide
ISBN 978-1-86144-165-2 £12.99

Drugs A Parent's Guide
ISBN 978-1-86144-136-2 £12.99

Dyslexia A Parent's Guide
ISBN 978-1-86144-138-6 £12.99

Bullying A Parent's Guide
ISBN 978-1-86144-137-9 £12.99

Epilepsy The Essential Guide
ISBN 978-1-86144-152-2 £12.99

Teenage Pregnancy The Essential Guide
ISBN 978-1-86144-139-3 £12.99

Gap Years The Essential Guide
ISBN 978-1-86144-169-0 £12.99

How to Pass Exams A Parent's Guide
ISBN 978-1-86144-140-9 £12.99

Child Obesity A Parent's Guide
ISBN 978-1-86144-141-6 £12.99

Applying for a Job The Essential Guide
ISBN 978-1-86144-180-5 £12.99

ADHD The Essential Guide
ISBN 978-1-86144-145-4 £12.99

Student Cookbook – Healthy Eating
The Essential Guide
ISBN 978-1-86144-146-1 £12.99

Stress The Essential Guide
ISBN 978-1-86144-147-8 £12.99

Your First Pregnancy The Essential Guide
ISBN 978-1-86144-158-4 £12.99

Special Educational Needs A Parent's Guide
ISBN 978-1-86144-149-2 £12.99

The Pill An Essential Guide
ISBN 978-1-86144-150-8 £12.99

University A Survival Guide
ISBN 978-1-86144-153-9 £12.99

Visit **www.need2knowbooks.co.uk** for the full range. To order our titles call **01733 898103**, email **sales@n2kbooks.com** or visit the website. Selected ebooks available online.

Need - 2 - Know Remus House, Coltsfoot Drive, Peterborough, PE2 9JX